THE FAILURE OF THE SEXUAL REVOLUTION

George Frankl

George Frankl was born in Vienna at a time when the socialist revolution which overthrew the Hapsburg Empire struggled to create an alternative society. He studied philosophy but soon became convinced that, for a proper understanding of cognitive processes, psychological factors must be taken into account and turned to the study of psychoanalysis and neurology. The Nazi invasion of Austria forced him to emigrate and he continued his studies in England and Canada. He is now settled in London where he practises as a psychotherapist. He has lectured on psychoanalysis and philosophy, edited a philosophical journal and was among the first to introduce the writings of Wilhelm Reich to a wide audience in Britain.

Frankl's works have been translated into several languages.

OTHER BOOKS BY GEORGE FRANKL

The End of War or the End of Mankind

The Social History of the Unconscious

Archaeology of the Mind

Civilisation: Utopia and Tragedy

The Unknown Self

Exploring the Unconscious

Foundations of Morality

Blueprint for a Sane Society

The Failure of the Sexual Revolution

GEORGE FRANKL

OPEN GATE PRESS
incorporating Centaur Press
LONDON

First published in 1974 by Stanmore Press Ltd.,
under their associated imprint: Kahn & Averill

First NEL Mentor edition 1975

Reprinted, with minor corrections, in 2003 by Open Gate Press,
51 Achilles Road, London NW6 1DZ

Copyright © 1974 & 2003 George Frankl
All rights, by all media, reserved.

British Library Cataloguing-in-Publication Programme
A catalogue record for this book is available from the British Library.

ISBN 1 871871 61 1

Cover image, from the 1975 NEL Mentor edition of
The Failue of the Sexual Revolution, designed by Jeremy Dixon.

The author gratefully acknowledges and thanks the following for permission to quote from copyright material:

Nova (IPC Magazines Ltd.): 'Monogamy' by Sally Vincent; 'Togetherness can destroy a marriage' by Charlotte Hopson.
Cosmopolitan: 'Bare Flesh is Big Business'; 'Now you have got me here what are you going to do?' by Ruth Dickson (1972).
She: 'The Man who came in with the coal' (1973).
Honey (IPC Magazines Ltd.): 'To the Beaches Where Bad Books Are Best' by David Robson (1972).
19 Magazine (IPC Magazines Ltd., 1973).
Probe Publications Ltd (1972): 'The New Sexual Demands of Liberated Women' and 'Can Liberation Lead To Lesbianism?'

Printed and bound in Great Britain
by Bell & Bain Ltd., Glasgow.

Contents

Preface	vii
INTRODUCTION	xi
1. REVOLUTIONS AND BETRAYALS	1
2. THE SCHOOL OF RADICALISM KANT, MARX, FREUD	6
3. THE PSYCHOANALYSIS OF ALIENATION	29
4. THE BUSINESS OF SEX	45
5. THE HALL OF MIRRORS JOURNALISM AND THE SEXUAL REVOLUTION	51
6. WOMEN'S JOURNALS	53
7. PORNOGRAPHY	79
8. ROMANTICISM	88
9. THE JOURNALISM OF PORNOGRAPHY	102

CONTENTS

10. POLITICAL PORNOGRAPHY   116

11. THE SEX-MECHANICS   122

12. THE LIBERATION OF WOMEN   134

13. AN EPIDEMIC OF MALE IMPOTENCE?   159

14. CONCLUSIONS AND BEGINNINGS   169

Bibliography   186
Index   190

Preface

People everywhere desire peace yet they kill each other in wars; they want to be free but constantly create authoritarian systems of society.

I first encountered this paradox as a boy, when the socialist movement of Austria collapsed in 1934. Having read *The Communist Manifesto*, essays by Victor Adler and other Austrian socialists, I took it for granted that the capitalist system had to be overthrown in order to eliminate poverty and social inequality. My parents and most people I knew were socialists, determined to make a just and humane society. But after a period of exhilaration and optimism a series of misfortunes befell the socialist experiment. The Austrian socialist party was liquidated by the semi-fascist regime of Dollfuss, the Spanish Socialist Republic fell victim to fascism (having been weakened by the intrigues between communists, Trotskyites and anarchists), and soon we became aware of the betrayal of communism in Russia. Finally Nazism set out to destroy all freedom movements and very nearly succeeded in doing so.

When I studied philosophy, particularly epistemology, I discovered that human reality is not merely a structure of events that exists independently of the mind but that reality hinges upon the mind that perceives it. This led me to ask how far social and political reality is created by human drives and, in particular, what force in man contradicts all conscious aspirations for peace and freedom. I began to realise it is not enough to emphasise that man is the product of his environment, but that human reality (inhuman as it often appears) is equally a product of man; that there is a psychological factor which makes a mockery of freedom and progress and imposes patterns of hostility, mistrust and power-worship upon all social structures.

The psychological factor operating in human reality became more clearly defined for me when I began to study psychoanalysis. The equation: sex negation-frustration-aggression threw light upon that apparently inevitable force sometimes termed the 'death wish' which can be seen operating in society and even in freedom movements. If there is anything constant in our society that underlies the economic and nationalistic forces it is the sex-negating compulsion of our culture. The anthropological speculations of Karl Abraham, Malinowski and Roheim, and the writings of Wilhelm Reich pointed to patriarchy as the source of sexual repression which generates frustration, pleasure-anxiety, distrust of the self and others. This also explained the authoritarian predisposition in individuals which perpetuates authoritarian society. Studies in social anthropology and of the behaviour of animals enlarged this view and, with amazing regularity, verified it.

The help I could eventually give to a limited number of individuals in my work as a psychotherapist did not remove my concern with the social problems, and I am convinced that the real contribution of psychoanalysis will emerge in its application to society. While I have for many years pondered about the apparently insurmountable difficulties of such a project, trying to clarify my ideas both strategically, as it were, as well as theoretically, a younger generation took up the slogan of sexual liberation in order to overthrow the taboos which create sexual repression and social oppression.

I have followed the new movement with fascination hoping that it might in some manner succeed where the socialist psychoanalysts of the twenties and thirties failed. Very soon however signs of betrayal and failure emerged. Established power groups and a great number of people who, for various reasons, were hostile to the establishment began to exploit the sexual liberation movement for their own purposes. Commercial interests and political pressure groups, sexual deviationists of all kinds, drug addicts and mystics, all began to impose their own image upon the sexual revolution causing confusion and degrading the intellectual clarity of purpose that guided its pioneers.

Once more I could see a revolutionary failure; once more the inevitability of the re-imposition of patriarchal patterns. I therefore decided to clarify the meaning of the sexual revolution and find out where it is going wrong, before a backlash of reaction completely defeats it.

I wish to thank all those who helped me to produce this book. I am particularly indebted to Mrs. Cynthia Maccoby whose support and lucid grasp of the subject matter both inspired and encouraged me. Her criticisms helped to clarify my purpose and prevented me from straying too far from the boundaries of my theme. I also wish to thank Miss Biddy Harling for introducing me into the mysteries of Women's magazines. And above all, I wish to express my gratitude to my wife who undertook the task of typing and re-typing the manuscript and had to put up with my indecisions and revisions. Her assistance in the production of the book was essential for its completion.

GEORGE FRANKL,
London, 1974 and 2003

Introduction

Psychoanalytic therapy is concerned with bringing about a sexual revolution in individuals. The sexual drives which have been repressed and forced to find an outlet in symptoms have to be brought into consciousness and accepted by the ego. In order to achieve the transformations necessary for emotional health the patient has to learn to acknowledge the sexual impulses which he has shut off from his ego; he has to be reunited with his libido.

The possibility of applying the lessons learned from the treatment of neuroses in individuals to the disturbances and conflicts of society became a central issue after the First World War. Foremost among those psychoanalysts who were deeply concerned with the social problems was Wilhelm Reich. He was quick to sense the relevance of psychoanalytic findings to society and he immersed himself in the struggle for social sanity with the same enthusiasm which he showed in his efforts to perfect the therapy of individuals. It became his ambition to connect the social revolution with the sexual revolution, and he set out to show that it is not only the economic structure of capitalism but also the psychobiological structure of sexually inhibited people that is responsible for the irrational behaviour of society. In his work as a psychoanalyst and later as a vegetotherapist he found that "only the liberation of the natural capacity for love in human beings can master their sadistic destructiveness."[1]

Reich tried to convince the Marxists that if they abolished capitalism and left the sex-negating structures intact, they would recreate an authoritarian society under whatever name it appeared. He was not alone in thinking that the social revolution must bring about a sexual revolution, that the overthrow of bourgeois morality would create a new morality of freedom. He became a member of the Communist Party, and in many articles and pamphlets emphasised the connection between sexual repression and social oppression. He founded the Socialist Society for Sex Consultation and Sexological Research and in 1929 opened, with a number of colleagues, sex hygiene clinics which gave free information on birth-control, child-rearing, sex education for children and adolescents. But the authoritarian character structure which he described in his books soon confronted him in the Communist Party. He was not only disillusioned and deeply hurt by the failure of the communists to understand his ideas, but before long he was slandered and attacked by them.

Reich had to learn by bitter experience that "the social struggles of today are between the interests safeguarding and affirming life on the one hand and the interests destroying and repressing life on the other hand ... it is a question of fully affirming and safeguarding the free and healthy life manifestation of the newborn, of children, of adolescents, women and men in an unmistakable manner or of suppressing and ruining them no matter with what ideological alibi."

(It is often forgotten that after the Revolution there was an upsurge of interest in psychoanalysis in Russia, with psychoanalytical centres opening in Moscow and other big cities. It became anathema to official thinking a few years later under the impact of Stalinist authoritarianism.)

Reich's work provided the foundation for the unequivocal understanding that freedom is not possible while a sex-negating character structure prevails in individuals and in society.

Psychoanalysis is a radical procedure or it is nothing; it aims to go to the root of a patient's conflicts however much this may be resented by his ego; it represents a searching and unflinching critique of many of his conscious assumptions about himself; it must question his rationalisations insofar as they serve to justify his defences against the libido. Equally a psychoanalytically orientated transformation of society that aims to go to the root of human conflict must necessarily be radical. Therefore a sexual revolution must be aware of its radicalism and we must differentiate between permissiveness and a revolution in fundamental sexual attitudes.

INTRODUCTION

To illustrate the concept of radicalism I shall draw attention to the three great representatives of European radicalism, Kant, Marx and Freud, and show the basic attitudes which they have in common. I shall also show the connections between Marx's concept of alienation and Freud's concept of repression and splitting.

One of the central questions I shall raise concerns the reason for the repeated failures of revolutions, for men's fear of freedom and why the superego always wins.

To illustrate the effect of the 'sexual revolution' upon the wider public I shall analyse its impact on journalism with particular reference to women's journals, commercial pornography and political pornography. I shall review the mechanistic attitudes to sexual freedom and the mechanistic type of thinking about sex, and also deal with the problems and inadequacies of the women's liberation movement.

While most of this book is necessarily critical of present trends, I shall endeavour in the last chapter to point to the real aim of the sexual revolution. This last chapter is bound to be incomplete but it will serve its purpose if it evokes new questions and stimulates discussion. I believe that it is necessary to point the way to the cure and to give some impression of what health or social freedom is like even if in the end the patient, i.e. our civilisation, has to discover it for itself. I believe that Marx was too hesitant in portraying what a socialist society should be. This omission could possibly be held responsible for the perversions of communism which might have been averted had he been more specific in defining his vision. However, I wholeheartedly agree with him about the need for an uncompromising critique of prevailing conditions. He wrote:

> "Since it is not for us to create a plan for the future that will hold for all time, all the more surely, what we contemporaries have to do is the uncompromising critical evaluation of all that exists, uncompromising in the sense that our criticism fears neither its own results nor the conflict with the powers that be."

It is right that at a time like this when so many changes have taken place, so many changes have failed and so many changes are still necessary, we look for the roots of human happiness. And the root of human happiness is love, and sexual happiness is the foundation of social happiness, for he who cannot find sexual happiness cannot love, and he who cannot love cannot build a good society.

Love without sexual happiness is impossible and the claims of love based upon sexual renunciation are fraudulent. Sexual happiness on the other hand is not possible without love.

A world which claims sexual freedom will have to rediscover an image of love and affection, not by spiritualising man at the expense of his body, nor by reducing him to a mechanistic system of bodily responses at the expense of his mind and emotions, but by recreating the consciousness of the whole person, where the bodily and mental faculties combine in the act of loving.

1. Wilhelm Reich: *The Function of the Orgasm* (Panther Books, 1966)

1. Revolutions and Betrayals

A completely new awareness has arisen in the second half of the twentieth century: the awareness of men's omnipotence. We are in a position to inflict absolute destruction upon life on this planet. While it is easy to say this, the meaning of this fact has hardly penetrated into our system of responses. This fact is so tremendous that all historical developments seem trifling in comparison. Before now, all manifestations of human power have been relatively benign in their limitations: in each instance, the danger that goes with power was limited, 'merely' people, classes, cities or empires were destroyed, but mankind as a whole was always spared. After each catastrophe, the thread of history was taken up again. We are the first men with the power to destroy the planet and to put an end to history. We are confronting not merely a quantitative change in human power, but a change in kind. There is not only more destruction available to us, but absolute destruction, and the mind of man conditioned by history is unable to grasp the end of history. The emotions are incapable of responding to a situation that has never before confronted mankind. Reason itself has few precedents to work on in order to grapple with this situation, and all our efforts to use past models of thinking to meet the demands of this new situation must fail.

There is, however, another type of awareness which is slowly penetrating our consciousness and that is that man himself and no one else is responsible for everything that is happening on the planet and in human society. The Gods who decided our fate are dead, laws of history or even laws of nature can no longer be held responsible for the affairs of mankind. The new awareness of human omnipotence does not merely relate to man's power of destruction but also to his creative power. Whether mankind flourishes or whether it destroys itself is the responsibility of no one but of man himself. The comforting images of an extra-human power which directs and decides his fate have disappeared, mankind stands alone and must take responsibility both for its survival as well as for the quality of life. Reason can no longer be concerned merely with knowledge and understanding but must learn to concern itself with making changes, with values and with the conceptualisation of aims. Reason must teach us how to live and it must teach us that survival is a human concern: that each man is involved in the survival of mankind.

A radical readjustment is necessary if we are to understand the dialectical jump from historical situations of partial danger to the complete and final danger to the existence of mankind. The radically new situation in which humanity finds itself requires genuine radicalism in thinking. Radicalism has become an obligation for survival.

But just at this point radicalism is losing its nerve. The uncompromising and critical evaluation of all that exists, the urge to understand reality in order to change it according to consciously held values is being replaced by petty rebellions and revolutionary posturings. At a time when reason is needed more than ever before, we find as R. Brustein observed, "a worship of naked slogans and raw emotionalism."[1] The search for a revolutionary alternative takes the form of a flight from reason, a regression to the irrational, while rationalism has degenerated into expertise in the service of the technological establishment. Rationalism used to be a revolutionary force but now appears as the enemy of revolution.

The faith in the capacity of reason to arrive at universal understanding has broken down in a proliferation of specialities, the contradictory fragments of knowledge each trying to mirror life. The specialists having evolved their own stereotypes of thought, and language can no longer communicate with specialists in other fields or with mankind. Specialisation has led to atomisation, rational scepticism to an erosion of meaning.

When reason has lost confidence in itself and people despair of understanding the world, then they regress to fantasies and

1. REVOLUTIONS AND BETRAYALS

infantilism. We are left with the alternatives: obsession with exactitude or romantic mysticism.

It can be said with some justification that the twentieth century is the graveyard of revolutionary hopes. There has never been a time in human history when so many gods have failed and betrayed those who believed in them. And now there is an acceleration of the cycle of belief and disillusion. In the past gods lasted for millennia, presenting an image of eternity and constancy. The ancient gods were replaced in the Age of Enlightenment by the God of Reason, representing man in the prime of life, strengthened by experience, wisdom and understanding. He lasted for a few hundred years and gave birth to a young God who saw his task not only in understanding the world but above all in changing it. He displaced the God of Reason, but still claimed to be his Son: Marx took the place of Galileo, Kant and Hegel.

The young god of revolution has died – to some of his believers it was Lenin's centralism that killed him – for others it was the shooting of the sailors in Kronstadt; to many more it was the emergence of Stalin's dictatorship and the show trials in the thirties that caused them to bury Marxism; other mourners appeared at the time of the repression of the Hungarian revolution or the military counter-revolution in Czechoslovakia.

The faith in the dialectics of history as a movement towards the classless society has been shattered by the traumas of the twentieth century and has given way to adolescent gods who have no consciousness of the past and no vision of the future. When there is a consciousness of history, the present is the link which connects the past to the future; without such an historical consciousness the present becomes a mere happening. The new gods, while assuming revolutionary postures, are no more than fashions, witless fantasies devoid of reason, experience and understanding – children play-acting at revolution. Their language is play-language, they use words to suit their impulses and, as children, feel no responsibility for the meaning of what they say. Meaning for them is only a symbol of what they happen to feel; each in turn is happy to speak his own language, not concerned with the common understanding mediated by reason. They are governed by the illusion of the omnipotence of impulses, the belief that through acts of violence the establishment will disappear or, that by negating it in fantasy, it will crumple up and vanish. Above all, like children, they forget quickly; their intentions and convictions are for the moment.

Reason can do no more than pretend to take the childish gods seriously. Impelled by the knowledge of its own failure and impotence, reason adopts a pose of benevolent sympathy with the tantrums of the child-god. But deeper down reason feels guilty about its own shortcomings and is desperately cynical with itself and with the world. Let the child-god take the stage when maturity has failed!

The child-gods however have parents who exploit them and make use of them in order to increase their own power – parents who allow the children to imagine that they are independent and omnipotent, yet advise them and finance them, encourage them and confuse them. Instant revolution is sold to the children, and the children are supported to play at radicalism. The child-gods are allowed to prance and shout, yet they are ruthlessly manipulated by vested interests. But the parents of the child revolutionaries, while thinking themselves very mature and wise, act and think on the level of primitive tribalism. They too are victims of the loss of faith, of the loss of nerve of reason and radicalism. When reason loses faith in itself, it becomes a tool for tribal compulsions, whether you call them democratic or socialist.

We may shrug our shoulders at the entrenched powers, and at the infantile pretences of pseudo-revolutionaries, we may be indifferent to our ideological waste-makers, but we should realise that without belief in a purpose that is both meaningful and appears rationally significant, man is unable to act and function coherently. At this point in history we must realise that the physical existence of our planet is dependent upon man's ethical and ideological choices and that a failure of belief must lead to the failure of human survival. Failure of belief for man is a failure of life, for man must project himself in front of himself either in the form of a god or a purpose in order to achieve a sense of direction and self-realisation. Man is a purpose-following animal

1. REVOLUTIONS AND BETRAYALS

and if he is deprived of an aim, anxiety will overwhelm him, and he will degenerate into self-destructive patterns of behaviour. We have passed through the age of anxiety ("angst" as the existentialists call it) and now confront the age of self-destruction. To alter this pattern we must again learn to think radically.

Man is the measure of all things, said Protagoras; he is the creator of all things, said Marx; and Freud asserted that the giver of all conditions resides in ourselves. Thus radicalism declares that man himself is responsible for his fate.

1. Robert Brustein: *The Third Theatre* (New York, 1966).

2. The School of Radicalism
KANT, MARX, FREUD

Radicalism stands on the tripod of reason, justice and love. The beginnings of radicalism in Europe are found in the rational revolution which intended to free the mind from its dependence upon superhuman knowledge revealed to man by special dispensation from above. It criticised the notion that knowledge derives from faith or from submission to a higher knowledge, be it in the possession of God, the Church, the State or any other authority. It taught man never to accept any concept as true without first subjecting it to rational examination; to accept neither revelation, dogma nor authority, nor to believe any statement unless it derives from the exercise of man's own rational faculty. The philosophy of rationalism subjected the processes of thinking and reasoning to searching analysis, culminating in the philosophy of Kant, and it was he who formulated the laws and rules as well as the limitations of rational thinking.

KANT

For millennia men have projected their own thought processes and their knowledge upon superhuman deities, ascribing to them knowledge and wisdom beyond human capabilities. Men regarded their projected thoughts as dogma to which they had to submit. This tendency of man to externalise his power and knowledge, and ascribe it to God, is deeply rooted in patriarchal society and in the Oedipus complex, as I shall show. It has dominated all traditional thinking, and rationalism was the first concerted effort to break this stranglehold upon the human mind. Kant, the greatest exponent of rational philosophy, set out to prove that the

2. THE SCHOOL OF RADICALISM: KANT, MARX, FREUD

human mind is in possession of certain fundamental, or innate, capabilities which transform sense-impressions into experiences, into understanding and knowledge. His critical philosophy is a systematic inventory of the powers, the characteristics and the possessions of the human mind. In every branch of knowledge Kant observes the contribution made by the human mind and attempts a critical evaluation of it. He examines the role which mental processes play and how they operate in science, mathematics, ethics, metaphysics and politics, and always draws our attention to the centrality of man and his reasoning processes in all forms of knowledge. He subjected the authoritarian traditions of thinking to a powerful critique and by so doing laid the foundations for man's liberation from superstition and dogma.

He set out to find the sources of knowledge and found them in the innate categories of the understanding; he also traced the source of all morality to the categorical imperatives which, like the categories of the understanding, are *a priori*, i.e. innate principles of our minds and common to all human beings. Thus in the field of ethics he also enjoined man to cease submitting to authority or dogma of any kind, and to employ his moral and rational faculties for the formulation of concepts by which judgments and actions can be guided. Man himself is to be the sovereign judge in the determination of good and evil.

While Kant can be regarded as the great representative of the philosophy of reason – which we can call the first leg of the tripod of radicalism – the second leg of the radical tripod was provided by Marx.

MARX

It is the vulgar view that Marx was only concerned with the economic basis of social existence, with the economic laws that govern society. Further, that the conditions of production of commodities, their ownership and distribution determine the character of a society as well as of human beings. This view of Marx is grossly misleading, as it ignores Marx's deep preoccupation with human authenticity. Those with a vested interest in economic change, or with upholding the *status quo* of the 'Marxist' state, ignore the centrality of the human being, the humanity of man, as put forward by Marx. Indeed, his concept of alienation, so fundamental to his whole analysis of capitalism, has its core in his concept of the free and authentic person.

To understand what one wants a society to be, or to be able to judge what is wrong with a society, one must consider what man is and what one wants him to be. Marx constantly returns to man himself as the creator of society and civilisation, and it was in the cause of human freedom, dignity and self-fulfilment that he subjected capitalism to a radical critique. Marx said: To be radical means to go to the root of things, and the root of human society is man.

Kant found the sources of our understanding and morality in the innate principles of our minds, which are common to all human beings. He affirmed that all reality, and our experience of it, is fashioned by our own mental faculties and is therefore a human reality. We do not need gods or dogmas to mediate between ourselves and reality; we ourselves are the creators and mediators.

While Kant connected the activity of the mind with awareness and understanding of the world, Marx connected the human activity of labour with the social and economic world of man. Like Kant, Marx conceived man's capacity for freedom and self-consciousness to be the fundamental human characteristic which separates him from animals. The practical construction of the object world, i.e. civilisation and society, is the confirmation of man as a conscious being. While Kant is chiefly concerned with the activity of the understanding, Marx is concerned with the activity of labour as the essential human quality. While for one it is reason and understanding that shapes reality, for the other it is human labour that does so. For Marx, the world of human reality is a product of human labour power, and if things go wrong with civilisation and society, then we should look to see what has happened to the work activity of human beings. While for Kant it is human error which is the object of his critique, for Marx it is the impoverishment of human beings under capitalism, their dehumanisation, which are his main concern.

Marx considered work as a living human function, probably

2. THE SCHOOL OF RADICALISM: KANT, MARX, FREUD

the most important of all human activities. He reminded the world that work, and not capital, is the source of economic processes. He observed that in capitalist society men do not work spontaneously and freely, that immense numbers of people were poor and miserable; that the reward received for their labour fell far short of the value of the products they produced; that the work they did was degrading both in its material conditions as well as in its human aspect. He saw how people were dehumanised in their work activity. When a worker sells his labour, the only commodity he possesses, to the capitalist, it no longer belongs to him but to the capitalist. Thus his work is taken from him and appropriated by the employer; it becomes part of the employer's capital. In this way the worker is estranged from his work activity – he becomes alienated from it. "Work comes to be external to man," says Marx, i.e. the worker does not affirm himself in his work but negates himself. The worker is, as it were, beside himself when he works and hopes to be himself only when he is away from work. One can see the modern worker's estrangement from his work activity in that "as soon as there is no coercion he flees from work as from the pest." [1]

We could say that Marx considered work to be a fundamental psycho-biological function of man. He describes work as a biological function insofar as man lives from nature, and since man is more universal than an animal so the range of nature from which he lives is more universal. Plants, animals, minerals, air, light, etc., are part of human life and activity. The universality of man appears in the universality which makes the whole of nature into his body as a direct means of life and as an instrument of his life activity. To say that man lives from nature means that nature is his body with which he must remain in a continuous interchange in order to live. Work on the biological level can be considered as a kind of symbiosis in which man, as a form of nature, inter-relates with nature as a whole. Work is life activity, productive life, life creating life.

Marx says: "Man makes his life activity itself an object of his will and consciousness. He has a conscious life activity. Conscious life activity distinguishes man from the life activity of animals. Only for this reason is his activity free activity." For Marx, the experience of this conscious activity, the spontaneous human self-expression in work as creativity is an inherent human capacity that characterises his species and in which he expresses and experiences his humanness. Alienated labour, instead of making his life activity into an expression or fulfilment of his being, converts it into a means for existence; self-fulfilment in work is negated, it is made irrelevant, and what is a fundamental source of self-expression becomes a means for survival. Insofar as a worker's labour power is exploited, he comes to exploit himself by regarding his work merely as a means. He splits his creativity off from himself and projects it upon the bosses, the manager, the expert, the scientist – all those who make the real decisions, as in the past he projected these qualities upon God and Kings, upon whom he then became passively dependent. Not only is he in this way alienated from himself, but he is dependent upon the authorities – those who bear responsibility and have the capacity for decision-making. All the important choices and decisions in life, all the real changes, are made not by himself but by *them*. Theirs is the power to change and make things; his work is simply a means for the fulfilment of their projects. No wonder the worker develops a mentality of least effort and escapes the treadmill as speedily as he can.

Besides the alienated relationship of the worker to his own activity we must, according to Marx, also consider the alienation of the worker from the product of his labour. In taking a job the worker enters into a contract whereby he sells his labour power as well as its products to the employer. The employer undertakes to pay him a price for his labour in the form of wages. Once a worker sells his labour power, he has no further claim upon the products of his work; they cease to have any relationship to him. The labour power as well as the product belong to the employer. Thus the worker's work activity as well as the product of his labour do not belong to him but to another man.

Private property is thus the result of alienated labour. The institutionalisation of private property, as Marx put it, becomes the realisation of alienation. While all pre-Marxist economists, and many even today, begin with the fact of private property as the basis of economics, they do not explain it but impute it in

2. THE SCHOOL OF RADICALISM: KANT, MARX, FREUD

some vague manner to 'human nature'. They assume that the motive forces of private property, the 'instinct' for possession and competition are innate in human psychology. Marx has shown that private property is not a fundamental or inevitable characteristic of society or of human nature. He questions what others took for granted, subjects it to examination and turns all previous economic concepts upside down by relating capital to the worker instead of relating the worker to capital; by seeing the worker's labour-power as the source of capital rather than capital as the source of work. He shows how private property emerged and how men have become slaves to wages and work a commodity, and maintains that an increase in wages means no more than a better remuneration for slaves.

Marx's concept of truly human needs, i.e. man's need to relate himself actively and imaginatively to others and to nature, to enjoy his skill and the imagination involved in the work process, the pride in producing an object, is fundamental to his approach to economics. Deprived of the enjoyment of the exercise of his creative faculties a man is a mere fragment of a man, mentally and physically dehumanised. Marx speaks of the possibility of man being "lost in objects" if they are not the conscious creation of productive beings, maintaining that capital is the manifestation of man lost to himself. The extraordinary situation arises that the work activity as well as its products which have been lost to man now confront him as capital. Capital is externalised and alienated work-energy and the worker is now completely dependent upon it. Thus it comes about that the whole edifice of industrial civilisation is alien to the worker. As he is merely a means for its operation, so it is no more than a means for his livelihood. The alienated industrial civilisation consolidates its rule over men by making them dependent upon it and men who have created it are its slaves. It assumes the power and the right to make decisions for its own purposes with little reference to the human beings who operate it. Despite all the proclamations of freedom and liberalism, industry has acquired an authority previously ascribed to God.

Once men alienate themselves from their own humanity and let it operate outside them, then the externalised human creative power will have complete authority over man, be it God or the machine. As the machine is a mechanical thing, a quantitative thing that is ruled by mechanical forces and numbers, it will impose upon men a mechanistic and quantitative image of the world, and of themselves; and the priests of the industrial system – the scientists, technologists, statisticians, the social and human engineers – see men in the image of the machine. Behaviourist psychology and recently, even moral philosophy, see people as significant entities only insofar as they can be measured and numbered as miniature machines. The human element – that which is not measurable and quantifiable – is considered as an awkward and undesirable factor in the equation, and theoreticians of the human and social sciences do their best to eliminate it from the scientific view.

Facts are supposed to rule the world and men are being conditioned and brainwashed to gear their thinking to facts, to adopt a factual orientation towards themselves and their environment, to eliminate such human aspects as value, imagination and emotion from their world view. It is quite conveniently forgotten that what we call facts, the edifice of our whole civilisation, are man-made, created by innate faculties of reason and by creative labour power. Man, alienated from the human and living aspect of the work process and isolated from the products of his labour, confronts his own creations as standing there outside, apparently independent of him, as facts. Facts therefore are alienated human creations, and the fact-worshippers, be they scientists, capitalists, bureaucrats, sociologists or psychologists, are a manifestation of an alienated state of mind.

Facts, facts, facts, shouted John Dewey, and man has built up a marvellously complex technology, but in the world of facts we are fast losing our humanity. Let us remind ourselves that the human world is not merely a conglomeration of facts, as behind every fact lies a mind, an intention, a symbol, an aspiration. A human being is not merely a fact but a universe of experiences, contradictory and puzzling, passionate and passive, dominating and enslaved, unpredictable, defying all the logic and quantitative rules that apply to the inanimate world. A human being contradicts all quantitative simplification, he does not fit into statis-

2. THE SCHOOL OF RADICALISM: KANT, MARX, FREUD

tics and computer logic. It is only to those psychologists who see fit to evaluate a man's psychological health by the standards of insurance statistics that man is a purely scientific object. The fact-worshippers would deny man his mind and his emotions if they cannot be measured statistically and electronically, or they say that mind can only be seen to exist insofar as its activities are measurable and quantifiable. Like the capitalist they are not concerned with the living processes of a man, they want to consider man as a fact, as an object, as a product and never as the creator of facts, objects and products, never as a being in whose imagination and by whose skill a world of facts is created.

As modern man is estranged from himself, from the products of his labour and from the industrial civilisation around him, so he is estranged from humanity. As self-alienation means alienation from one's reasoning processes and one's will and creativity, so it means alienation from mankind. His image of himself and of human beings generally is that of a thing, a commodity, to be bought and sold, to be used. Insofar as he sees himself as an exploited being, a piece of capital, he will view all men merely as beings who wish to sell themselves on the capital market for the highest possible price. For him all men are merely commodity bundles, as Erich Fromm has said. He has lost the image of the humanness of humanity – he has lost a genuine human consciousness. As he views the world as consisting of material and human commodities to be bought and sold, he will acquiesce in a commodity-orientated life, he will come to regard it as 'natural and inevitable', as a manifestation of 'human nature'. The processes of capitalist relationships reproduce themselves in the consciousness of man and, in turn, reproduce a society that reflects an image of man as the seller and buyer of work, talent, aspiration or fantasies. Everything has its price. A man's ability is merely a commodity. It has to be sold in accordance with the demands of the market.

It is into this world that the sexual revolution has been propelled and, as I shall show, has become inevitably twisted and deformed by it.

The alienation of man from his humanness as well as from the world goes deeper today than even in Marx's time. The commodity-orientation and the thingification (reification) of human beings has proceeded apace. While the technological universe closes in upon us, the humanness of the world recedes. We are dominated by a seemingly alien power, by a world of things and facts and we have forgotten long ago that it is we who make the facts of our world. This world of facts and things appears no longer as a human world, it is void of human meaning and men are not able to see themselves reflected in it. Karl Jaspers has written: "What in all the millennia of human history and pre-history no God has been able to do for man he has done for himself ... and he shrinks back in alarm from the void he has created." Jaspers is concerned with the problem of whether man can preserve his identity in a world dominated by a giant technological and bureaucratic apparatus of his own creation yet alien to him: "The price we pay for progress is anxiety, a dread of life perhaps unparalleled in its intensity. That the sufferer may feel himself to be nothing more than the lost point in empty space inasmuch as all human relationships appear to have no more than temporary validity."

The power of alienated technology with an aim and purpose of its own outside and independent from the human producer is, however, not limited to the capitalist system. People have built more and better machines to produce more efficiently, and the machines make them into slaves, or kill them, whether they are the machines of capitalism or of the so-called socialist states.

Marx's effort to reunite man with his creativity and with humanity has failed. Marx himself has become a commodity, a victim of the laws he analysed. The bureaucracies that operate in the name of Marxism are perfect examples of the dehumanising and depersonalising processes that go with man's self-alienation. Alienation of the worker is not confined to capitalism, as we are finding out. A state bureaucracy that claims ownership of the means of production can appropriate a man's labour power and the products of his labours, and alienate him, just as ruthlessly as any capitalist.

The myth of socialism as nationalisation of the means of production and distribution is probably one of the great frauds of history. What Marx saw as an inevitable transition in the revolu-

2. THE SCHOOL OF RADICALISM: KANT, MARX, FREUD

tionary struggle to expropriate the expropriators, the temporary takeover by a socialist state of all industry and finance as a step towards the establishment of socialism, has been frozen into permanence and has itself been given the name of socialism. "Marx and Engels were unable to foresee that their own doctrine might become the ideology of a technocratic élite intent on imposing its authority upon the workers, in the name of – socialism!" [2]

Modern societies have been successful in their efforts to rationalise the conduct of human affairs by subjecting them to rules, regularity and hierarchical command to suit the requirements of technology and have vastly increased the power of bureaucracy. It should have been foreseeable that a large centralised bureaucracy could assume the same alienating powers over people as capitalism. It is quite obvious that once a bureaucracy appropriates human labour-power and establishes itself over people under whatever pretext, it acquires the same power as that held by capitalism. Just as you can alienate your labour in the service of capitalism and create your technological prison, so you can alienate yourself under a bureaucratic system which, just because it claims superior authority, will divest you as an individual of your humanity.

Here we come to one of the mysteries of human nature, namely its capacity to dehumanise itself in the name of humanity, to deny itself freedom in the name of freedom, to lead a compulsive existence in the name of liberalism. What was wrong in Marx's thinking and what has gone wrong with the efforts to overcome man's alienation?

Many critics of Marx have complained he imagined that the rational awareness of the economic processes of a society suffices to cause men to act decisively to put an end to their exploitation. They claim economic considerations are not enough to provide the moving force for collective action, that a sense of a spiritual purpose is required, an ethic that fires the imagination.

Marx was perfectly aware of this problem, and from what I have already said it can be seen that Marx was by no means merely concerned with greater economic rewards for the working masses but with the abolition of the indignity of the worker.

There has been much discussion recently as to whether Marx

was fundamentally a moralist, whether Marxism can be interpreted as a system of moral philosophy. There is no mistaking the fact that his thought-processes are decisively governed by basic value judgments. We cannot, however, see Marx's writings as a system of ethics. He does not start with an analysis of the supreme Good or the criterion of right conduct and, what is more, he was adamantly opposed to raising these questions. For instance, in *The German Ideology* he writes: "Communists in general preach no morality ... they do not make moral demands upon men to love one another, nor to be egoists, etc. On the contrary, they know full well that egoism, as well as self-sacrifice, is in certain circumstances a necessary form of the self-assertion of individuals." We can assume that Marx's acquaintance with moral philosophy was limited and it is doubtful whether he ever made a thorough study of Kant's moral philosophy, although Kant's concept of human autonomy must have been familiar to him. Karl Popper believes that Marx deliberately avoided an explicit moral philosophy because he hated preaching, and he argues that Marx's writings contain an ethical theory by implication and this he calls an historical moral theory or "moral futurism". This term is used to distinguish Marx's position from that of Hegel which, according to Popper, holds that whatever historically is – is right: Marx's moral futurism holds that whatever inevitably will be in history is for that reason right.

One can object to this formulation on two counts. First, by drawing attention to the fact that Marx did not, in the least, hate preaching. There are many instances in Marx's writings and in his lectures where he unashamedly adopts a prophetic stance and displays a burning intensity of conviction. Secondly, there is nothing to indicate that Marx morally affirmed the future world revolution on the ground of its presumed inevitability. While yet a young man he became convinced of the desirability of the revolution and then embarked, as Robert Tucker pointed out, on a life-long effort to prove that it must come. The conviction, as happens in all great undertakings, preceded the analysis. The messianic aspect of Marx's thinking has often been pointed out, and it has much relevance to his ethical orientation. The concept of human fulfilment through history assumed an aim towards

2. THE SCHOOL OF RADICALISM: KANT, MARX, FREUD

which history moves. The fulfilment of man's potential lies in the end of history, the messianic fulfilment at the end of time, when all previous history is seen to be a sort of pre-history, a preparation for man's full self-expression and fulfilment.

In the Jewish concept of history and its messianic climacteric the profane merges with the spiritual, it is fundamentally transformed or revolutionised through the spirit. The profane is not replaced by the spirit but transformed by it. As Moses Hess, the teacher who converted the young Marx to socialism, wrote: "The end of days is not as other people misunderstood it the end of the world but rather the accomplishment of historic development and the education of humanity. We are at the eve of the sabbath of history and we should prepare ourselves for our final mission."

Marx's concept of the classless society, where oppression and exploitation, those two great barriers to men's self-realisation, are overcome, has obviously much in common with the messianic vision. For Marx, the spirit which descends upon man and overcomes his estrangement from God, from himself and from his fellow men, overcomes his alienation from himself, from the products of his labour and from society, is man's consciousness of his humanity, the consciousness of history and class consciousness. Class consciousness, in particular, is the vehicle by which men can overcome the divisions between them by making them conscious in the first place. The working-class, being the chief victim of alienation and oppression, is the vehicle through which the historic force of the revolution is to be realised. It is the agent of history. Through the class consciousness of the working class and its revolutionary purpose, history realises itself. In this respect we can see Marxist ideology as a kind of historical ethics where history is the movement towards man's realisation of his humanity. "A doctrine which demonstrates no more than the likelihood of a planned (and centrally controlled) society taking the place of an unplanned one, is not a 'critical theory' in the original Marxian sense of the term. The latter stands and falls with the belief that human action can bring about the end of 'pre-history'. Unless this claim is made good, the socialist revolution cannot be regarded as a radical break with the past." [3]

Marx gave man and in particular the working-class an image

of their humanity and of their role in history. The "species-consciousness" of man was to be manifest in the class consciousness of the worker and of the intelligentsia who ally themselves with the workers against their exploiters. By doing so they would put themselves on the side of historical development, and bring about a revolution to initiate the classless society where every creature is able to live and develop unrestrainedly according to his own determination and his inner calling; where every man lives and acts as an end and no man is ever a means for another.

How did a philosophy devoted to the affirmation of freedom become authoritarian? Marx showed how alienation transforms man's own activity into an alien power which confronts him and makes him dependent upon it. It did not take long before 'Marxism' itself became alienated; the revolutionary will of the masses which was to transform society became externalised into laws of nature and history that operate independently of man and confront him as historical and economic determinism. In order to appeal to the alienated masses of capitalism as a political doctrine, 'Marxism' adopted alienated models of historical inevitability which assure the collapse of capitalism and the victory of the proletariat, ignoring the subjective (human) determinants of social transformation.

The movement towards a vulgar, historical and economic determinism already emerged in Marx's time and made him exclaim that he was not "a Marxist". Rosa Luxemburg was one of the few communists to realise that a revolutionary movement which is based upon an authoritarian ideology is bound to create an authoritarian society, that its success would mean a defeat of the philosophy of Marx.

We can see a shift towards natural and historical determinism in Engels, in Lenin's concept of the Communist Party as a sovereign instrument of the revolution, in his semi-authoritarian centralism against which Rosa Luxemburg protested in vain, and eventually in Stalin's megalomaniac image of himself as the personification of the laws of history.

Marx despised men who let themselves be reduced to slavery, whether it took the form of religious or social authoritarianism or in the reduction of man to a commodity. He did not,

2. THE SCHOOL OF RADICALISM: KANT, MARX, FREUD

however, ask: Are the millions of working individuals willing and able to take their responsibility for social progress? As Reich pointed out, Marx made a miscalculation which all freedom movements have made, a miscalculation based upon the assumption that as the social process is fundamentally determined by the working masses, they, given self-consciousness and leadership, will be able to change society. Marx did not understand that not only the masses of the population but humanity as such is afraid of freedom, that there exists in its psychic structure a need for submission to authority, a predisposition to what Kant called heteronomy.

And here we come to the third leg of the tripod of radicalism: that of Freud and depth psychology. Marx could not have understood the processes in man which caused every freedom movement, every aspiration for peace and human co-operation to fail. It was left to psychoanalysis to uncover the roots of this human paradox.

Let us recall the logic and the development of the radical tradition. For Kant it was the intellect innate in man which creates forms of perception and of understanding and which is responsible for our concept of reality and all our experiences within it. Marx maintained that what we call reality is not merely an edifice transmitted to us by our categories of thinking, but the creation of human labour. It is man's humanity insofar as it expresses itself in work-activity which is the producer of human reality. In a different language and from a different approach Freud maintains that "the giver of all conditions resides in ourselves."

FREUD

Psychic forces which are independent of the conscious mind and act in the unconscious parts of the person determine our thinking and our actions, says Sigmund Freud, and to this we can add: they fashion and form our society, they are responsible for its rules, rituals and taboos. To consider social and economic forces without the active psychic and emotional forces operating in them is meaningless. If we take the proposition seriously that the roots of human society lie in man, then it is preposterous to ignore the functions of the human psyche. We cannot limit ourselves to the consideration only of economic forces which operate in society but have to consider the psychic, i.e. subjective forces in man which might be held responsible for the creation of exploitive economic systems and also for the attitudes of submission and servility, for man's incapacity for real freedom.

The radical tradition upholds the conviction that man is not a passive being helplessly dependent upon external forces but a being that, through its reason, its work and its emotions, creates the human reality. It affirms the autonomy of man against the older world views based upon heteronomy.

Freud's discovery and exploration of the human psyche and, in particular, its unconscious elements, not only paved the way for the understanding of emotional disease and symptom formation, but also for a comprehension of the emotional and irrational bases of human society.

Even if Freud had never lived, attentive minds would have been drawn towards the exploration of that something in man that seems unchangeable and mocks all civilising efforts and all the pretences of reason and morality, and remains the real driving force of action. The nineteenth century produced thinkers who in a philosophical and sometimes poetic manner anticipated the discovery of the unconscious. One of the great thinkers of the nineteenth century, the much maligned and misunderstood Arthur Schopenhauer, developed a system of philosophy that proclaimed the primacy of the will and of the instincts over mind and reason. He pursued reason to its ultimate source and found it to reside in the will which he saw as the core and the central foundation of all that lives. He constructed a concept of the will in nature of which man is but an individuation, as he called it, to which the intellect is a secondary manifestation, its servant and its pale illuminant. He used the concept of the will in a very wide sense, much wider than either Kant or modern thinkers would permit. He recognised the will as being largely unconscious and the conscious mind as well as our reason barely more than its tool. His pessimism had its foundation in his awareness that the claims of primacy, which reason upholds for itself, are an illusion. In his extraordinary essay *Transcendent Speculation on Apparent Design in the Fate of the Individual*, he sets forth that "precisely as in a dream it is our own will that unconsciously determines objective destiny, everything in it proceeding out of ourselves and as each of us is the secret theatre manager of our own dreams, so also in reality there is but a single essence, the will itself that dreams with us our fate. We actually ourselves bring about what seems to be happening to us." His whole complex of thought is even to the presence of the sexual paradigm a philosophical anticipation of psychoanalytical conceptions.

I am not certain how well Freud knew Schopenhauer's philosophy, but according to his own admission he refrained from studying Nietzsche for a long time, so as not to be influenced by his powerful insights into human psychology. Indeed, in Nietzsche, a disciple of Schopenhauer, one finds on almost every page premonitory flashes of Freudian insights. Novalis and Kierkegaard in their own and different ways had a comprehension of unconscious forces that defy reason and control the world and the mind of man.

While the genius of Schopenhauer recognised the power of the will in nature and in man operating unconsciously and determining reality, he was led to pessimism by his awareness of the subordinate role of reason. Freud in the tradition of Kant was determined to employ reason in order to arrive at a conscious understanding of that which was previously unconscious, and at least partially to bring light into what was previously darkness. The life of reason could not be content with a retreat before the powers of the unconscious determinants of human life. The rationalism of Freud has the quality of high sophistication. It does not simply assume, as the earlier rationalists like Descartes and John Locke did, that man is a rational being, but posits a rational capability whose task it is to apply itself to what was unknown, to the non-conscious and irrational areas of the mind. Where id was shall ego be, said Freud, or to paraphrase him – Where compulsion reigned there shall freedom be. The frontiers of the unconscious are to be pushed back by the expansive forces of consciousness and understanding.

That part of man which has been alien to him shall be reunited with him, and we do not deal here only with man's labour and its products but with a far wider dimension of the human being, with the very core of man's psychological and mental processes. Freud quotes Napoleon as saying that politics is our fate, but he says that we must recognise that it is man's own unconscious that determines our fate.

Freud came to his research into the unconscious through his study of neurotic symptoms. Before him, these were considered – if they were rationally considered at all – to be due to somatic or biological degeneration, or lesions of the nervous system. They were considered as neurological pathologies to be treated electrically or chemically, as indeed in our own time the so-called empirical psychiatrists are still wont to treat them. Freud himself worked as a neurologist of distinction before he went to Charcot and Bernheim, whose methods of hypnotic therapy drew his attention to the various layers that operate in the mind apparently disconnected from each other. Charcot and his pupil, Pierre Janet, developed the theory of double consciousness and of the dissociation of the personality which they derived from the observation of hypnotic phenomena. They concentrated upon the psychic nature of neuroses and were convinced there was an area of the psyche that was not conscious but could influence human conduct. On his return to Vienna Freud began to practise as a psychotherapist and gradually gained the impression that many of the symptoms which patients manifested meant something; that they had a symbolic significance by which a hidden part of the patient's mind endeavoured to express something. Soon he began to decipher the symbolic meaning of these symptoms.

The experience Freud gained in his work enabled him, together with his friend and colleague, Dr. Breuer, to formulate hysteric symptoms in the following manner: "The regular and essential content of a recurrent hysterical attack is the recurrence of a psychic state which the patient has experienced earlier, in other words, the recurrence of a memory. This memory moreover relates to a highly charged emotional situation which is given no outlet by the patient in his normal life. The patient seeks to forget an experience which strongly aroused his emotions, or

2. THE SCHOOL OF RADICALISM: KANT, MARX, FREUD

repudiates and replaces an intention or idea. Thus the psychic acts which are being repressed enter into the second consciousness and return to the surface, and gain their expression in the form of an hysterical attack." All hysterical symptoms, Freud wrote in 1892, are impressions that have failed to find an adequate discharge. The symptoms thus are a symbolic expression of emotions and ideas of which the patient wishes to know nothing about – which he represses from his consciousness.

The question now presented itself: What are the drives and memories which are repressed and what agency in ourselves does the repressing?

It was not long before Freud almost reluctantly had to acknowledge that the impulses and memories which are subjected to repression from consciousness were almost invariably of a sexual nature, followed frequently by destructive and aggressive urges.

We may remark here that it was rather fortunate that Freud was not a very good hypnotist, that he felt a disinclination towards the authoritarian form of hypnotic induction practised in his time and, consequently, discovered the method of free association. This method, while not as 'efficient' as the hypnotic method, allowed a much wider range of observation into the function of the human psyche. It gradually disclosed the processes of resistance, transference, the function and mechanisms of dreams, the distinction between the various layers of the unconscious and, above all, it enabled the patient to trace the sources of his forbidden sexual fantasies and experiences back to childhood. The more thoroughly the psychogenesis of a symptom was explored, the more definitely did the associations of the patient lead back into the past and ultimately to early childhood. In this way Freud discovered many aspects of the sexual life of children which were in opposition to traditional views. It led him to the formulation of his theory of infantile sexuality, and the laws of its development and transformations.

The analysis of patients' childhood memories showed that sexuality is not limited to genital sexuality, that children are not sexless, as had been assumed, but that there exists in the child a wide spectrum of sexual drives and that, at certain periods of the child's development, certain sexual drives become dominant, i.e. attain primacy over the others. While one can speak of the child as being sexually polymorphous with a whole host of sexual interests existing at the same time, one observes that certain sexual interests predominate at certain stages of development. Freud learnt that sexuality is not an instinct that manifests itself in a particular form but is more like an energy that undergoes many transformations in a person's life and that, furthermore, these transformations develop with great regularity in all the individuals he analysed. This regularity of transformations emboldened Freud to formulate a law of sexual development which has since found ample confirmation in the psychoanalysis of children and adults.

When Freud discovered the processes of sexual development he also discovered that they can be disturbed, that a person may be arrested in his sexual development and, in consequence, may suffer from a fixation upon a certain sexual primacy. The development of sexuality – the transformation of sexual primacies – is greatly influenced by environmental factors, such as the parents' attitude to sexuality and the child's capacity to achieve gratification and discharge of its sexual needs. If any of the sexual needs of a child are blocked or inhibited, the unfulfilled libido will continue to demand gratification and will spill over into the next stage of development, thus creating a whole host of problems such as association of genitality with dirtiness or aggression. Fixations upon a certain stage of development are decisive factors in the aetiology of neurotic or psychotic disturbances and are of major importance in the development of a person's character.

It was one of Freud's greatest achievements to discover that sexual energy, or libido as he preferred to call it, is involved in all the major bodily functions and is not confined to the genitals, that the bodily processes have a sexual dimension and that sexual disturbances can create somatic disturbances. I have in my own work found that even the internal organs have a sexual cathexis. For instance, the respiratory, gastric and urethral organs, including the kidneys and gall bladder, can become sick if the libido connected with them is disturbed. Reich has drawn atten-

2. THE SCHOOL OF RADICALISM: KANT, MARX, FREUD

tion to the sympathicotonic processes of the musculature, to muscular tensions and rigidities in states of anxiety, while the effect of psychic shock or anxiety upon the circulatory system is well known.

Freud showed that the activities of the lips and the mouth, the exercise of the musculature, the sensations of the skin and of the body periphery, the urethral functions, the anal activities, even looking, listening, touching, tasting and thinking all have an erotic component and that genital sexuality is only one of the many aspects of the libido, albeit one of the most important. We can thus conceive of sexuality as an energy which permeates the living organism, and seeks discharge or expression in a wide range of psychic and organic activities. In the development of an individual, one form of expression after the other seeks primacy. That the other areas of sexual interest do not disappear during the reign of genital primacy is shown by the fact that in normal adult love-making the earlier erotic activities such as sucking, kissing, looking, smelling, etc., play an important part and genital pleasure and fulfilment is the culmination of all sexual needs. Every fulfilling sex act of a mature individual is, as it were, a recapitulation of his sexual development.

This brings me to another important aspect of Freud's thinking – his observation of pleasure as a discharge phenomenon. The discharge of a drive, i.e. its fulfilment, creates a pleasure experience, while the inhibition or blocking of a drive creates unpleasure or anxiety. This results in the extraordinary phenomenon of pleasure anxiety. The repressed sexual urge in its demand for an outlet attacks, as it were, the repressing agency, threatens to break through its defences and causes it to experience anxiety. Pleasure is not merely an experience that accompanies sexual discharge but is in itself a discharge activity, that is to say the experience of pleasure in itself discharges sexual stimulation. Another discharge activity is consciousness. Pleasurable urges constantly strive to be accepted by consciousness which belongs to the peripheral area of the mind. Drives do not seek to have only somatic and motor discharge but also mental discharge through consciousness. The block set up by the repressing agency is both a somatic block in the form of muscular rigidity and tension (which Reich calls the body armour) as well as a mental block creating a rigidity of mind and an inhibition against conscious awareness of internal as well as external stimuli. We can thus speak of a bodily as well as a mental armour.

What then we must ask, as Freud had to ask, is that agency which does the repressing, which blocks the avenues of discharge? This question forced Freud to arrive at a structural model of the human psyche.

He taught that the agency which is responsible for the activities of repression and blocking is none other than the ego. The ego can be seen as that part of the psychic structure that regards itself as the constant self, the identity of self that is continuous in time and uniform in character to which stimuli relate and which reacts to stimuli, which selects and co-ordinates reactions. The ego is the seat of a person's awareness of himself; it is the centre to which everything relates, that experiences itself as permanent in the flux and variety of sensations. Even though a person's own body and his state of mind can change, even while the ego may be aware of these changes, it perceives itself as constant. Out of the thousands of stimuli pressing for discharge from within a person's somatic and psychological system, and the thousands of stimuli from outside demanding responses, the ego selects those which are in keeping with its own character. It is the co-ordinating and selective apparatus endeavouring to keep a measure of psychic equilibrium.

It used to be customary to equate the ego with consciousness and to equate consciousness with mind. I think, therefore I am, said Descartes; it is my ego that thinks, that is conscious both of myself as well as of the world around me. Mind and consciousness used to be equated to differentiate them from natural or somatic processes. The fact however could not be overlooked that mental processes are, to a large extent, dependent upon somatic influences and on their side have the most powerful effect upon somatic processes. If ever human thought found itself at an impasse it was here in the mind/body problem, as Freud remarked. Body and mind were conceived as two separate categories, and the body/mind problem remains one of the problems of philosophy and psychology.

2. THE SCHOOL OF RADICALISM: KANT, MARX, FREUD

It was one of Freud's most daring and controversial claims that mind cannot be equated with consciousness, that being conscious is not the essential characteristic of the mind, that consciousness is only one aspect of it and that this aspect is more often absent than present. He claimed to show that the essential mental processes are unconscious and far from excluding the unconscious, he saw it as the most important part of the mind. Unconscious mental processes constantly strive to enter into consciousness and, as I have said, it is the function of the ego to screen the unconscious and select those drives to which it concedes the right to enter consciousness. The psychic energy which generally remains unconscious Freud calls the id.

The id is in direct contact with somatic processes, takes over instinctual needs and gives them mental expression or form. It is not ruled by logic nor by the laws of contradiction. Contradictory impulses can exist in it side by side, it has no concept of space or time or order. It has no values, no sense of good or evil, no morality. "Instinctual cathexes seeking discharge is all that the id contains," says Freud. It is the bridge, the most fundamental link between instinct and mind in man, but it has no organisation and no unified role, only an impulsion to obtain satisfaction for its needs. The ego only allows those id processes to come into consciousness which are acceptable to the standards which the ego sets itself. The ego also transforms id drives by means of symbolisation and displacement processes to make them acceptable to consciousness.

One can say that the ego is, from a genetic point of view, that part of the psyche which has developed from the id and which has been modified by its proximity to the external world. It serves the purpose of receiving stimuli and protecting the organism like the cortical layer with which a living substance surrounds itself. The ego has taken over the task of presenting the external world to the id and so protecting it. For the id blindly striving to gratify its urges in complete disregard of outside forces could not otherwise escape destruction. The ego develops a reality system, a reality test, by means of which it can eliminate such stimuli from the id which contradict the demands of reality. The ego interposes between desire and action the delaying and selecting factor of thought. In this way it dethrones the pleasure principle as the only guide-line of responses and substitutes for it the reality principle which promises greater security and greater success. In order to cope with the stimuli from within and from without, and to integrate them into a sense of order within which perception and consciousness of reality can develop, the ego has created the concepts of time and space. Time, as Kant has rightly said, is the category of internal awareness, whereas space belongs to the category of external awareness. The ego creates these categories or concepts, but also co-ordinates them. Causality, mass, extension, the law of contradiction are also the creations of the ego. The ego has to perceive the instincts as well as control them by subordinating them to a larger organisation, thus giving them a place in a coherent unity.

It is the task of the ego to safeguard the sense of continuity and coherence of the self. The task of the ego is not an easy one, as it is constantly bombarded by conflicting drives and impulses. Its standards and aims can be subjected to doubt and uncertainty and sometimes it relinquishes its post and becomes flooded by unconscious or infantile drives in which case it falls victim to psychosis or, if it only partially relinquishes its post, to neurosis. In any case, it needs a powerful guide to give it direction and the function of guiding the ego is exercised by the superego. This guide often fails grievously as its own severe demands and expectations in turn can cause the ego to despair. The superego often holds up strict norms of behaviour and tries to enforce them upon the ego without regard to the difficulties presented by the id and the external world.

1. Karl Marx: *Economic and Philosophical Manuscripts* (Lawrence & Wishart, London).
2. George Lichtheim: *Marxism* (Routledge & Kegan Paul, 1961).
3. *Ibid.*

3. The Psychoanalysis of Alienation

In any attempt to understand the motivations of social behaviour the study of the superego must take pride of place. The superego is not merely a psychic faculty that operates in individuals, it also has a social dimension which manifests itself in the authoritarian social establishment. In other words there is not merely an individual superego but also a social superego and we can say that social authority, in whatever form it appears, is the institutionalisation of the superego.

Political and economic power is not an adequate explanation for man's submissiveness to authority, for his fear of freedom, nor for the morality of self-sacrifice. Furthermore, while authority claims to speak in the name of morality and reason, its demands are all too often irrational and immoral. While the intellect has no difficulty in observing these contradictions, men have not been able to rid themselves of the compulsive powers of the social superego. A psychological analysis of the authoritarian social structure must supplement the economic analysis given by Marx, and as the superego plays a vital role in the authoritarian system of society, I shall try to give a short explanation of its development in the individual. We shall follow this up by tracing its manifestations in society and will be able to see that oppression is only possible if men have a predisposition to be oppressed, that alienation is only possible if economic forces can utilise a psychic readiness in men to be estranged from themselves and from the products of their labour, and that the quest for sexual freedom must fail if the reigning superego creates guilt and anxiety.

I hope to show that the conversion of man's creative activity into a commodity is based upon the compulsion of making a gift offering of himself and his product to the superego, to God and the social authority. We shall also notice the paranoic structures of patriarchal societies and their compulsions to wage wars.

Let us retrace our steps. I have said that the id does not know morality or order, that its sole aim is to find discharge for its impulses and the attainment of pleasure. The same applies to the infant. Its main preoccupation lies in the gratification of its needs and while it is not an unstructured mass of libido – as some people seem to assume – it does not know nor care about reality, being only concerned with the experience of pleasure and the avoidance of pain. At the earliest stage of an individual's life there is only the perception of tension and pleasure, an inside something. Soon the awareness of an object as a source of pleasure or anxiety creates the awareness of an outside something and, with the differentiation of self and object, a self-image appears in the form of the narcissistic ego which is entirely self-seeking, i.e. is dominated by the pleasure principle. It demands pleasure and love from outside objects and has no awareness of the effects of its own actions upon the objects. (One sometimes wonders whether humanity has ever outgrown this stage.)

Soon, however, the child learns that the parents react in certain ways to its own impulses and activities and that some actions are disapproved of and punished while other actions evoke approval and love, i.e. that some actions and desires are bad and others good. Good is what arouses love and pleasure responses in the parents, bad is what arouses the withdrawal of love, separation or punishment. The child experiences anxiety when it encounters its parents' disapproval, and pleasure at their approval and gradually becomes aware of their attitudes to its own urges and actions, incorporating them into its own ego, and it enacts towards itself the punishment or approval which it has learned to expect from its parents. The prohibitions set up by the parents remain effective even in their absence. The parental image here becomes part of the ego – it is incorporated into the ego and becomes the superego. The superego takes the place of parental restrictions and like a constant internal watchman observes, guides and threatens the ego.

While Freud in his early writings assumed that the superego

3. THE PSYCHOANALYSIS OF ALIENATION

emerges with the Oedipus complex, later on he and other analysts, particularly Karl Abraham and Melanie Klein, traced back superego formations to much earlier stages of the child's development. We can now say that the superego goes back to pre-genital stages and that in fact, every sexual primacy develops its own superego. We can speak of a transformation or evolution of the superego culminating in the Oedipal superego which becomes the dominant superego in a person's character. Thus, the superego is not a single internal presence of the parents' attitude towards the libido but rather a stratified system of negations and prohibitions, most of them unconscious. The part of it which is conscious, or preconscious, is usually called the conscience. The difficulty about the conscience is that it is only the tip of the proverbial iceberg, a rationalisation of a large range of taboos and anxieties. There is furthermore not only a punishing or frightening superego but also a good and loving superego.

It is one of the discoveries of depth analysis that a child is intensely aware of the role it plays in the emotional life of its parents: how much the parents love it, whether it is desired and wanted by them or rejected and regarded with indifference. The mother who loves the child experiences the child as a source of pleasure, feeling pleasure in the child's pleasures. She, in turn, is experienced by the child as a good mother and the child feels itself to be good. The mother who suffers from pleasure anxiety will feel anxiety in the child's pleasure experiences, the child will be a source of anxiety to her, her anxieties will be transmitted to the child and the child will feel her to be a bad mother and will feel itself to be bad.

No mother, however, is always good or always bad. She may be good in respect of some of the child's impulses or actions and bad in respect of others, i.e. enjoy and approve some impulses and censure and punish others. She may be inconsistent in her attitudes towards the child's feelings according to her own mood and, if this inconsistency is very pronounced, it can confuse the child. If the mother pretends love and affection but feels indifference or hostility, if for instance she assures the child that she loves and cares for it and the child feels she is unloving or indifferent, then a double-bind situation arises where two opposite attitudes emerge and this leads to a split in the child's superego which can result in neurotic indecision, varying in range of intensity to schizophrenia.

Freud repeatedly stressed that the internalised parental images are not realistic but are usually highly distorted. The study of these distortions is perhaps one of the most important tasks of psychoanalysis as they are at the root not only of personality disturbances but also of the irrationality of societies and cultures. The distortions of the superego images are due to the processes of splitting and projection.

SPLITTING, PROJECTION AND SYMBOLISATION

As I have written earlier, parents who adopt a censorious and repressive attitude towards the child's libido impulses will cause the child to experience pleasure anxiety. In order to reduce anxiety the child will repress its pleasure sensations. It will estrange itself from its own feelings as if they did not belong to it, as if the ego were to say: I don't experience anything; I am quite dead or at least harmless; it is something else or somebody else who is doing the experiencing, the experience is outside me. This process represents the unique human capacity of self-splitting and one important aspect of this splitting process is the projection of the repressed impulse or feeling upon an outside object, which is then imbued with the characteristics of the split-off self.

In our culture, or more precisely, in the patriarchal culture dominated by sex-negation, most of the sexual feelings and impulses of the child encounter parental censorship and denial. The libido denied turns into aggression. The aggressive impulses in turn become repressed by the ego, they are made ego-alien and are projected upon the parents. The parents in this way acquire an aggressive or frightening image and this, in turn, is introjected to become the punishing and frightening superego. For instance, the oral libido, if frustrated, acquires an aggressive component and becomes oral-aggression, oral-cannibalism directed towards the breast – the child will have fantasies and impulses of attacking and devouring the breast. Oral-cannibalism is of course stimulated

3. THE PSYCHOANALYSIS OF ALIENATION

also by the growth of teeth, but its predominance in a child is not an automatic biological process, as has been assumed by many psychoanalysts, but the result of frustration and anger. If oral-cannibalistic impulses predominate in the child, the ego will dissociate itself from them and the child will project its oral aggressive impulses upon the breast, thus creating fantasy images of a breast that attacks the mouth.

In this way we can see how the aggressive part of the id fuses with the superego and appears as a threat to the child, causing it to experience intense anxiety or terror. Thus the reactions which the parents arouse in the child will, to a great extent, be projected upon them and transformed into symbolic imagery. Symbolisation plays an important part in the representation of superego images. A symbol presents emotions or attitudes in terms recognisable to the senses; it is the transformation of drives and emotions into visual images. Every emotion subjectively experienced finds its visual representation by means of a symbol. As the patriarchal family generates a great amount of aggression in the child, the superego symbols, which are the projection of the child's emotional reactions, will be largely aggressive and threatening.

The oral sphere, with its incorporating, sucking, biting, cannibalistic aspects, creates symbolic presentations of all these activities in figures with sharp teeth and claws, wild animals with devouring mouths, crocodiles and dragons with large teeth, birds with threatening beaks, distorted angry faces, witches, etc., besides fantasies of a good loving mother, the smiling fairy who protects the child from the witch.

The urethral libido creates fantasies of being carried away by waves, of being lured into the sea, fears of drowning, etc.

In the anal stage fantasies of slippery floors covered in dirt, overfull chamber pots and lavatories, faecal figures and snakes threatening the body openings, and dirty devils, proliferate.

Needless to say, these ghosts and demons populate the preconscious fantasy life even of adults; they become powerful in neurotic situations and completely dominate our thoughts in psychotic states. The child tries constantly to abreact these demons and monsters in play-activities and in mime. By imitating the monsters the child can, to some extent, overcome his fears of them. He masters them in endless forms of play-acting spookery, or in the spontaneous outbursts of frenzied miming which are so puzzling to adults. (Some avant-garde theatre is to a great extent on this level.)

These childish fears are still with us as we grow up and no amount of rationality completely obliterates them from our minds. Drama and ritual are efforts to master these monsters which lurk in the unconscious mind and frighten the ego. In our time of 'secular commonsense and rationality' the monsters invade the very fabric of our society and its ideologies.

THE AUTHORITARIAN SUPEREGO

When the child becomes five or six he enters the genital stage of the libido, and sexual urges, as we generally understand them, become powerful and dominate the libido. With the strong stimulations experienced in its genitals it will develop an interest in the genitals of the parent of the other sex. The boy feels the urge to relate sexually to his mother; he wants her for himself and to get rid of father. As father stands in the way of the boy's sexual fulfilment with mother and denies him his genital satisfactions, the boy's aggression will turn against father. He will have impulses to get rid of him, kill him or castrate him. But as the boy also loves his father he will repress these destructive urges from his ego and project them so that the father will acquire a threatening image.

With the advent of heterosexual genitality the pre-genital monsters and spooks give way to a more personal image of the superego. However this image will still retain certain pre-genital components as no one is actually free of pre-genital fixations. Thus the aggressive father-image can be a devouring cannibalistic monster (Baal, Gog and Magog) who wants to eat the boy, the sinister figure with the knife (the surgeon, the scientist or the Jew), who threatens to castrate the boy.

It is characteristic of the projected images that they are split between the good and the bad representing our desire for love and our aggression. They know our thoughts and see what is in

3. THE PSYCHOANALYSIS OF ALIENATION

our minds. The good demons, fairies and deities know of our good intentions, they take our side and guide us against the evil in us, and in the world around us. The struggle between these two sides of our nature and their representations in the spirit world is probably the most important aspect of all mythological drama.

The parental superego is also split into the bad and the good. In fact one can say that the Oedipal superego is split in four ways, as can be seen in the pre-conscious fantasies of individuals and in the mythologies and religions of pre-patriarchal culture. There is the good God who loves and cherishes the child, who makes the child feel good and loved; there is the angry God who, while still a good God, is outraged by the nasty aggressive inclinations of the child; then there is the devil, the projection of the defiant and sexual urges, the evil, cunning, scheming Mephisto, who threatens the boy and tempts him away from his love for God. And finally there is the good devil who shows us how to enjoy ourselves, who can dance and sing and recite ribald poetry, the perennial Rabelais and Picasso, the élan vital – Pan. He is the innocent devil who laughs and is curious, the begetter of the arts and sciences, the cheerful philosopher whom Nietzsche tried to emulate and whom Russell admired.

We can see that the projections which emerge in the Oedipal situations of patriarchy retain many aspects of earlier phases, many characteristics of the childhood of mankind, and of the individual. The sexual rivalry with the father during the period of the Oedipus complex retains aspects of oral aggression and anal defiance. Fantasies of incorporating father's penis play a large part in the fantasies of the Oedipus complex, and they can be of a loving kind in the form of identification or they can be destructive: the good incorporation and the bad incorporation. The former create images of the father who wants to be accepted by us so that we can learn through him and acquire his knowledge – the foundation of learning and identification. And then there is the destructive devouring, the mutilation of father. Oral aggression which has previously been directed towards mother and projected upon her and made her the witch, is now directed towards father. As the exercise of oral aggression indicates power over the object by incorporating and possessing it, so the boy will want to attack and incorporate father and, in turn, develops images of a father who wants to devour the boy.

Defiance of father can evoke anal-defiance and dirt-defiance; the boy may become a 'dirty devil' refusing to cleanse himself. The 'dirty devil' has affinities with freedom movements, with socialism, anarchism and liberalism, which defy the authoritarian God and show tolerance to dirt, to the child's primitive needs, which support the arts and the lower classes (who in the pre-conscious fantasies of societies are regarded as the unclean ones). However, despite the complex interaction of Oedipal with pre-Oedipal drives, the rivalry with father will in the Oedipus situation of patriarchy acquire a central significance. The father will, as I wrote earlier, become omnipotent; he will be there to threaten and punish; he will inhabit the boy's dreams and fantasies; he will be a threat to the boy and punish him for transgression. He will be here, there and everywhere, in his head, in his school master, among the bigger boys, the grown-ups, the boss, the policeman, the judge and the king. He will be lurking in the churches and official buildings and, above all, he will be up there in heaven behind the clouds. In the boy's dreams he will bar doors and paralyse him, he will take women away from him, he will make him crash on his bicycle or in his motor car. The boy will retaliate with fantasies of punishing and castrating him, outwitting him, beating him, tearing him to shreds and taking *his* woman away from him and having intercourse with her while the ghost looks on in rage and the boy has a frightened ejaculation, an ejaculation without orgasm, or an orgasm of terror. But in the end he will have to propitiate the father-god in order to free himself from anxiety, and the most significant form of propitiating him is the restitution and glorification of father.

The oral-aggressive component of the Oedipus complex, with its cannibalistic urge to devour father, is transformed into symbolic fantasies and rituals whereby the boy allows father to devour him. He submits to father and propitiates his anger by self-sacrifice. The urge to eat father is transformed into a ceremonial of being eaten by him. The enormous range of ritualistic killings, of totem feasts and of initiation rites gives wide expression to the process of restitution.

3. THE PSYCHOANALYSIS OF ALIENATION

Morality as we know it in our Judaeo-Christian culture is the morality of being devoured by God, of entering into him and living through him. The Jew enters into a covenant with God by giving God his penis symbolically in the act of circumcision. By the act of circumcision the boy promises never to defy God nor set himself apart from him. He ensures that God, having power over the boy's penis, will never forsake or hate him. By the covenant of circumcision and the undertaking to study and obey God's laws the Jew has removed the need for any further masochistic sacrifice. He has entered into an indissoluble bond with God. God may be angry or dissatisfied with the Jews, his sons, but God will never forsake them. The Christian version of their relationship with God is different. The pagan masses to whom the new Judaism (Christianity) appealed, had not entered into a covenant with him; they were not circumcised and did not know the Torah and God's commandments, but they recognised in the crucifixion of Christ a familiar pagan rite. In the new Pagan-Judaism men projected their hatred of God upon an alter-ego figure, who took upon himself all the repressed aggression, all the sins of mankind and by his sacrifice redeemed mankind.

Those Jews who lost their trust in God when the Romans occupied Jerusalem and entered the Temple, and the pagan millions who never knew the Jewish God, had to seek his love and forgiveness through self-sacrifice and the glorification of suffering – the ritual of sacrifice replaced the Jewish covenant with God. God became a stranger, evermore angry and threatening and only the mediation of the sacrificed figure of Christ, the split-off alter-ego of man, could evoke his mercy and forgiveness. The ego offered another part of itself to the devouring God. Christ became that part of the human ego which had to be eaten up by God so that he could love man again. We have here a complete return of the fantasy of sacrifice to the angry God.

PATRIARCHAL PARANOIA

Up to now I have spoken of the projection of repressed urges upon the parental figure, the father-God. There is, however, another type of projection which has become increasingly important with the secularisation of society. As the main function of the ego is to achieve a good relationship with the omnipotent father-symbol, we must endeavour to reduce our aggression towards him and thus limit the amount of aggression projected upon him, in order to make him appear less aggressive. Thus in patriarchal societies men project a great part of the hostility they feel towards their superego authority upon other tribes or nations who are then depicted as the enemies of the superego. The repressed id projects its aggression not only upon the paternal image but also upon other tribes, who then represent aggression and hostility towards their own superego, their own nation or tribe.

It is as if man's preconscious self says: O God, it is not I who am hostile to you and disobedient – it is the others; it is they, the outsiders, the foreigners and the strangers who wish to destroy you; let them be sacrificed so that I can have your friendship and love. And as it is the others who threaten your power and glory, let me fight them in your name and sacrifice them to you so that I can partake in your glory and in your love. In this way the repressed libido and forbidden aggression is split off from the group and appears as group-alien; it emerges by means of projection outside the group and is symbolised by the 'others', the alien tribes, nations or classes. The superego thus has to be protected from the attacks of the others, it has to be upheld and glorified, made more and more powerful and defended against the enemy. So patriarchal groups are bound to be paranoid, for the hostility against the denying superego must be made ego-alien, or group-alien, in order to uphold the integrity of their own group.

Besides the paranoid assumption of aggression in the others, there is the image of the others as representing all the repressed sexuality, i.e. others are sexually dangerous, they want to rape the motherland or all the women in one's tribe; they are dirty, or low, etc. Needless to say, this fear of the others and the glorification and defence of the superego never leads to peace or relaxation, for the id denied constantly creates an energy of aggression against the denying superego, the ego constantly projects this upon the others, and the others will always remain a threat however much the tribal superego is defended. If there

3. THE PSYCHOANALYSIS OF ALIENATION

were no enemies they would have to be invented, for the aggressive urges must be projected outwards. Alien groups or nations are needed to release the pent-up aggression which cannot be expressed towards its own superego.

Thus we can understand the curious sense of virtue felt amongst citizens who hate foreigners, the 'others', because hatred shown towards the others tends to guarantee loyalty to the group superego. Submission to the group superego and aggression towards the foreigners is a patriarchal virtue.

WORK, PRODUCT AND COMMODITY

We have spoken of the projections and splitting processes which can be seen to be at the core of religions and wars. Projections take still another form, namely the projection of the repressed libido upon material things. The mind which gives the libido a dimension in imagery by which the libido perceives and visualises itself also becomes attached to material objects and they are transformed into symbols. I have written above of the myths and dreams, the images which exist in the world of the imagination – the spiritual world of demons, witches, monsters, fairies and gods – and here I want to deal with the myths and dreams presented in the material structures of civilisations as symbolisations of the libido that have been split off from ourselves and externalised.

Marx said that the whole of human reality and all civilisation is an externalisation of human labour-power. We can now say that civilisation is the externalisation of the libido, manifested in spiritual and material symbols.

Civilisation is the drama of the unconscious enacted in reality. The house we build and the garden we cultivate are symbolic of the womb, the vagina, of the pleasure of playing with and caressing the mother, the woman, the earth. But the house we live in and the garden we enjoy are simultaneously symbolic and real. Multiply a thousandfold the symbolisations and you get civilisation.

The activity that creates material symbols is work. Work is

the link that connects fantasies, symbols, imagery with material objects. Work transforms images into reality. From the earliest beginnings of the human species the making of tools did not originate in economic considerations – these are the by-products which generally reinforce the activity – but they originate in man's capacity to symbolise urges and impulses, to transform a material object into a symbolic artifice through work. Tools are symbolic presentations of man's organic impulses, they are his claws, teeth and muscles, not merely extensions of his organs, but their externalisations. The feel and the pleasure of an organic function is transferred to a material object and this material object takes over the function of an organ.

As I have written in *The Social History of the Unconscious*, man is an organism that can externalise itself – it can project itself outside and the projected self can exist as a separate entity. Man can be in himself and outside himself. What is more, he can think himself from outside himself (what Hegel called the objectivity of the spirit or the God who can have a view of man is a manifestation of self-externalisation). *Man can feel himself and recognise himself in the things he creates, but he can also be alienated from them – become a stranger to them.*

Man objectifies his fantasies, images and his creativity and, having done so, he needs to reunite himself with them. This takes place by means of identification with the externalised or objectified self. Identification is introjection. Man projects himself into the world and then introjects his projections, i.e. identifies with them. If we cannot achieve identification with the externalised self then we are alienated from it – a stranger to the world and to ourselves. It can be seen that I differ here from Marx who equated externalisation with alienation, repeating Hegel's error. Externalisation is a human characteristic par excellence and is responsible for all civilisation and culture. Alienation from the projected self – the things man has created – is a manifestation of sickness, of individual and cultural crises and Marx was right to consider this sickness to be prevalent in capitalism where the working masses, having externalised their labour-power, are then deprived of its products and become dehumanised strangers in the world they have made.

3. THE PSYCHOANALYSIS OF ALIENATION

In patriarchal authoritarian societies the externalisations are taken over by the superego. Everything men create becomes a gift-offering to the authoritarian establishment and the more men produce, the more powerful the establishment grows. In a technologically-orientated society the wealth produced enhances the power of the state and the ruling class whether it be the property-owning class or the ruling bureaucracy.

Man feeds his superego in order to be accepted by it, and to alleviate his guilt. The ritual of feeding father with the products of labour "through good works for the glory of God" is an essentially Jewish/Protestant-Puritan form of worship which has been dominant in Europe since the seventeenth century and created the impetus for industrial society and capitalism. The older Christian images of self-sacrifice through Jesus in piety and meekness, the need for salvation from the sins of this world and from the pleasures of material wealth of course still linger on. The gold that is sinful to man can glitter in the churches for the glorification of God. The Protestant church is more austere, and the secular Protestant establishment is satisfied with the accumulation of "brass".

The superego devours both the worker and his product – the goods produced by him go to the superego's representatives in society and are then transformed into capital. Capital is the accumulation of the wealth produced by the workers and taken from them. Marx has called capital the governing power over labour. No wonder he exclaimed: "The worker is related to the product of his labour as to an alien object. The more the worker expends himself in work the more powerful becomes the world of objects which he creates, the poorer he becomes in his inner life and the less he belongs to himself. The worker puts his life into the object and his life then belongs no longer to himself but to the object."

He did not understand the psychological processes by which the object-world becomes part of the establishment – he did not understand that this object-world is appropriated by the superego which demands man's self-sacrifice.

It is this patriarchal compulsion to submit to the superego which defeated Marx and all freedom movements. Perhaps Marx had a pre-conscious awareness of these processes when he spoke of God as the Being who absorbs man's creative power: "The more of himself man attributes to God the less he has left in himself." He spoke of God as an externalisation of man, and constantly contrasted the rich human being, the rich internality of man, with the poverty of man who has become alienated from himself. Marx did not know about pleasure anxiety and splitting processes, nor did he know about guilt, repression and the need to propitiate and restitute the paternal superego.

The patriarchal superego is insatiable and men remain slaves to it. As guilt is reproduced from generation to generation, men are impelled to make gift-offerings of themselves and their creations to the superego. Every invention and creation of human genius is a sacrifice to the establishment Moloch.

In technological patriarchal societies the products of labour are the property of the ruling class, they become an ingredient of capital and are transformed into commodities. When men are alienated from the experience of creative work and from the products of their labour, when the essential aspects of life have become commodities, then men feel compelled to turn to the market to regain some part of their alienated self. Purchase is the modern worship by which men can reunite themselves with their split-off, alienated selves. Modern man subjects himself to the market economy in order to reunite himself with what was taken from him. Advertising becomes the litany – the umbilical cord by which men rediscover what they have lost.

The shopping precinct is the modern place of worship – the essence of modern civilisation. Where cathedrals once stood and men gathered to worship the visible or invisible God, now the shops are places of worship and the commodities displayed take the place of the Altar and the Cross. Communion is now through the cash nexus and buying and selling the ritual of salvation.

But it is not only material goods which have become commodities, for, under the authority of the market economy, dreams, works of art, talent and inspiration are the commodities of the entertainment business, ideas and thoughts – commodities of publishing.

3. THE PSYCHOANALYSIS OF ALIENATION

SEX AS COMMODITY

And now sexuality has become a major commodity. The sex merchants have a huge market among sexually repressed and starved people. While in earlier periods this market was restricted by Christian inhibitions, now that the sexual revolution has released us from the compulsions of secrecy, sexual commodities are flooding the market and are becoming the most profitable area of capitalism next to the market of aggression – the armaments industry.

We can see here the paradox of the sexual revolution and its failure in its own terms.

Wilhelm Reich wrote in 1935: "Capitalist class morality is against sexuality and thus creates a conflict between human needs and society. The revolutionary movement eliminates this conflict by a sex-affirmative ideology and then giving it practical forms by legislation and a new order of sexual freedom. Authoritarian social order and social sexual repression go hand in hand, and revolutionary morality and gratification of the sexual needs go together." In 1944 he wrote: "The necessity of a radical change in conditions of sexual living has already permeated general social thinking and continues to do so at an accelerating pace." Reich postulated that the whole social structure of capitalism, being based upon authoritarian morality, depends for its existence upon self-negation which deprives the masses of sexual spontaneity, creates awe and fear of the ruling class and upholds the hierarchic class system. With the creation of a sex-affirmative orientation capitalist authoritarian society would become an anachronism and give way to human co-operation, social freedom and personal spontaneity. Repression would give way to self-regulation, economic exploitation to work democracy.

The sexual liberation was intended to free men from the fear of the libido and from guilt; also from the authoritarian structure of their personality and the authoritarian society, thus putting an end to men's submission to the oppressors. It assumed that freedom to love would create freedom from fear and from aggression; that freedom from sexual repression would create freedom from social oppression. The sexual liberation was intended to be a catalyst for social change that would go to the roots of authoritarian society and transform it. But the sexual revolution has got stuck in an advocacy of permissiveness and has not touched the deep structure of society; it has only produced attitudes of defiance and rebelliousness which emphasise a negative dependence upon the superego establishment. Liberation from pleasure anxiety has been transformed into a worship of alienated sexuality in the form of a commodity. The superego is managing quite nicely to use the superficial aspirations of permissiveness for its own purpose by making a business of it, and our 'revolutionaries' are falling for the deception.

4. *The Business of Sex*

Instead of being the catalyst for radical social change, the sexual revolution serves as a catalyst for business, opening up a new territory – a whole new continent for commercial exploitation.

Through commerce and science the old antagonism between the libido and the social establishment becomes obliterated: the establishment absorbs its enemy. Sexual fantasies have now become commodities.

The more liberated sexuality is, the more people are free to pursue their sexual needs, the more they can be exploited by the market for profit. There could be no better salesmen for the sex business than the promoters of sexual freedom.

The spectacle of man's submission to the superego in patriarchal societies is undergoing a new and unexpected transformation. While Marx was chiefly concerned with the conversion of man's material products into commodities, we are now faced with the transformation of man's emotions and his sexuality into commodities. When sexuality is no longer overtly repressed then it can become a commodity, openly bought and sold.

All previous history was concerned with the disparity between man's material needs and their availability; it was a history of scarcity. When men's lives were governed by the struggle to obtain material goods necessary for life, it was the role of the establishment, by possessing the means of production and the raw materials, to provide them. As long as men sold their labour they would obtain a measure of reward from the accumulated products held by the property-owning establishment. While the establishment was in possession of all the goods desired by the masses, they could be persuaded to work hard so as to obtain a share of the social wealth. The establishment had to see to it that the working classes would not be too satisfied, for that would promote laziness, and at the same time not be too dissatisfied, for that would lead them to lose faith in their masters, creating social unrest.

The commercial and industrial establishments had to promote the virtues of frugality, for the most important task of the economic system was to get the masses to work as hard as possible and to expect as little as possible in return. The religion of Christianity and Puritanism was ideally suited for this purpose. While Christianity preached the other-worldliness of rewards, i.e. the real rewards would materialise in the next world, this world, being steeped in sin and guilt, could not provide the happiness men dreamt about. Puritanism preached the virtues of hard work as a form of masochism for which man would be rewarded not so much by material gratification but by a sense of virtue and righteousness in the eyes of the Almighty. The virtue of hard work and the denial of worldly pleasures was the great myth that kept the masses for long periods in a state of relative contentment and productive quiescence. Even poverty and suffering could be justified by pointing to the imperfections of this world and to the salvation in the Kingdom to come; the poor will inherit the world – after they are dead.

When industry got over the hump, as they so beautifully call it in economists' jargon, when it became capable of producing more than enough material goods and the main problem was how to get them sold, then the virtues of frugality became counterproductive. In order to provide the vast productive capacity of modern technology with new markets the emphasis shifts from frugality to the virtues of consumption. The creation of a market demand to satisfy not only the material but also the emotional needs of the masses has become the new task for capitalist economy.

A vast industry has developed, devoted to the production of drugs that promote emotional satisfaction or protection against anxieties. Depressant and anti-depressant drugs, mood changers and consciousness changers are now big business. If you are depressed the establishment can help you; if you are desperate about your place in a dehumanised society, the establishment can

4. THE BUSINESS OF SEX

revive you, cheer you up, stimulate you, free you from anxiety, make you optimistic or transfer you mentally into a better world. When you suffer from a debilitating sense of impotence, meaninglessness and powerlessness, there are the amphetamines that can stimulate your nervous system and give you confidence, alertness and energy: benzedrine, dexedrine, methedrine, steladex, drinamyl among others are all available for you. On the other hand if you need quietening down, if you are tense and restless, then the barbiturates and tranquillisers will give you that peace of mind which, in previous times, could only be achieved by hard work and religion.

If you feel empty inside yourself and life appears meaningless, if your mind lacks vision and imagination, if the world appears colourless, uninteresting and dreary, then there are the weeds: cannabis, marijuana, hashish, pot, grass and whatnot. And if you really want to experience life in its colourful and dramatic fullness there is LSD and assorted hallucinogens – and you can make a religion of them if you wish.

The emotion engineering industry remains very busy. There are a great number of books written dealing with the statistics of this industry concerning the numbers of people who are its consumers, the millions of prescriptions made for them, their percentage of the whole medical industry, the capital and the firms involved.

The conflicts and anxieties of the repressed libido are exploited by the industrial establishment, and the population, from the respectable suburbanites to the revolutionary drop-outs, have their little altar of drugs by which they worship the miracles of the chemical industry.

Another, older emotion industry is, of course, the entertainment industry. Eros in his battle with Thanatos, Prometheus in his struggle with Zeus, have created entertainment and drama all through the ages to provide release for the libido denied. There was never a libido-negating establishment that did not find itself ridiculed, outwitted, cheated; there was never a sex-negating morality that man could not defy and best in popular art, music-hall, vaudeville, theatre, satire, drama, music and dance. Men always had entertainment to obtain release for the inhibited libido, to gain momentary revenge against the powerful negators. But now the entertainment industry has almost completely taken charge of men's need for libido discharge and catharsis. The superego provides opportunities of discharge for Eros but keeps the discharge apparatus, the pharmaceutical industry and the entertainment industry, under its command. Drugs, theatre, cinema, literature, journalism and the electronic industry that produces radio, hi-fi and television – all cater for the market of emotional needs.

In the economics of post-scarcity, puritanism is replaced by the cult of hedonism, and the establishment is there to gratify it. The sexual revolution has now gone one better. Sexual repression and puritanism is no longer necessary as long as the worship of the establishment continues.

The superego establishment is now in the extraordinary position to say to the masses: give up your inhibitions, have as much sexual pleasure as you like, we can sell you all the stimulants you want, we can teach you the arts of full sexual satisfaction and we can supply you with advice about sexual etiquette. You are no longer subject to the rules of sexual scarcity; now we enter into the age of material and sexual affluence, and business and science can supply the goods. You will continue to be dependent upon the establishment but this is an establishment of affluence and permissiveness. There are now hardly any restraints and the more you follow your desires, the more you will consume our products and the happier we shall all be.

A cynic would say that if the sexual revolution had not emerged it would have had to be invented by capitalism, and the manner in which we find it operating today guarantees the *status quo* of the social order. What Marcuse has called the one-dimensional man has no vision or need of an alternative of a transcendent order, but finds his expectations of happiness contained within his social establishment. When society grants, indeed encourages, consumption and emotional and sexual pleasure, then rebellion against the social order appears meaningless. If frustrations of the libido still make their appearance against all realistic expectations, then they do not lead to a desire for social change or revolution but cause neuroses and 'neurotic' discon-

4. THE BUSINESS OF SEX

tent. Whether the neurotic discontents manifest themselves in individual neuroticism or in irrational social behaviour, such as delinquency, criminality or adolescent rebellion, is all the same, for they can be cured by the medical and pharmacological industry, by psychiatrists, marijuana and LSD.

Today the sexual industry neutralises a revolution which threatened to dethrone the superego, to put an end to authoritarian repressiveness and class society; what was meant to be the revolution to end repression and oppression has become the latest prop of the establishment.

The question immediately presents itself: how is it possible for the superego to maintain its reign without sexual repression and without fear? Let us remember that the permissiveness of the affluent society does not remove the deeper layers of repression, it merely covers them up. The appearance of permissiveness represses the repression, so to speak, and creates a moral doublebind: on the one hand the superego is kind to us and, on the other hand it says – appreciate my kindness – or else. The failure of the sexual revolution is a failure of radicalism, and attitudes of thought which intended to go to the root of things are being defeated by the attractions of permissiveness and pseudo-rebellion.

Herbert Marcuse, one of the best of our radical thinkers, placed his hopes in the student revolution, as did his teacher, the courageous and generous philosopher Theodor Adorno, who died of a broken heart over the brutalisation and political intrigues that overtook the student revolution in Germany.

There is, however, another way in which the libido can attempt to find an outlet, and that is in mysticism and the cult of the irrational. As bourgeois culture has adopted rationalism with science and technology, people who wish to reject it will, in some cases, make the attempt to discover the gratifications of a pre-rationalistic culture. When the rest of the world is trying to imitate Western civilisation in order to escape poverty and backwardness, a number of people in the West refuse to accept the culture pattern of their establishment and look for cultural images that have long ago been discarded. Identification with African or ancient Indian cultures, with American Indian and Tibetan mysticism, is fashionable among those who search for an alternative. A great rummaging in the historical lumber-room of defunct cultures is taking place. At the same time individuals who wish to dissociate themselves entirely from the prevalent superego in order to gain greater freedom for their id, try to deny the ego itself – they seek experiences untrammelled by reason, reality and consciousness, maintaining that consciousness stands in the way of real self-experience. The cult of irrationalism and of preconscious symbolism has found its way into literature, the theatre and mystical ideology. Even in certain types of psychiatric ideology we find an attempt to elevate schizophrenia into a kind of psychic health more authentic than the sanity of the 'adjusted' person. It is obvious that these attempts to discover an alternative mode of experience are bound to fail, for it is neither possible to discard the cultural acquisitions of the Western world, nor the ego's preoccupation with reality.

When the ego feels impotent to deal with reality, it often regresses to pre-conscious areas of the psyche, into neuroticism or some kind of psychosis if certain infantile fixations are powerful enough, or it can attempt to regress culturally into a primitive type of imagery. This is a typical example of pseudo-revolutionism, as it is no more than a retreat to an alternative experience through an evasion of reality. I consider this to be not merely socially futile but harmful, for, if these revolutionaries had their way, actuality would be left in the hands of the superego establishment and the reactionaries. In their retreat from reason and their search for surreal experience, they weaken human autonomy and leave real decision-making to others.

While the regression to mysticism and primitive culture-patterns presents an interesting phenomenon of our time, I will not enter into a discussion of its role in the sexual revolution but will concentrate upon those aspects of it that can be seen to be in the mainstream of the movement.

5. *The Hall of Mirrors*
JOURNALISM AND THE SEXUAL REVOLUTION

Journalism provides not only information but a viewpoint by which to approach the world. It is the superficial book of life; it reflects man's consciousness of himself and of his society unconcerned with any deeper motivations. It mediates between isolated men and the world and allows them to participate in it vicariously. Journalism has, at all times, reflected social norms and presented the interests of various classes and strata of society. Newspapers and journals express a two-way movement between society and its members. On the one hand they mirror the attitudes and expectations of the superego establishment and on the other hand reflect the attitudes of members of a society towards the establishment. (The subtle way in which the papers reinforce the superego norms, while giving catharsis to discontent, is a fascinating psycho-social study.)

The sexual mores of a society are mirrored in its journals, and as sexuality has been openly adopted as a way of life, this fact is brought home to the citizens via its news media. When repression deprives people of contact with their natural needs, when images of desire and desirability become blurred, then people are dependent upon the establishment to provide a self-image. It is as if the ego were to say: I am not allowed to have a conscious image of myself as a natural sexual person, so I depend upon the superego to present me with an image of what I am supposed to be so that I can imitate it and model myself upon it.

To be sure, every culture propagates an ideal image of man in keeping with its expectations and its myths. However, with the disruption of traditional images and religious values, people have turned to sociology to rediscover the laws and forces which underlie the life of society. Sociology as a scientific discipline was meant not only to base social processes upon scientific laws, but also to provide men with an image of themselves and a new sense of social orientation. A whole new language, with its own clichés and symbols, was created to take the place of the old litanies.

The failure of sociology to displace the old irrationalism is well known, but where sociology has failed, journalism has succeeded. Journalism can be considered as a personalised form of sociology, a medium for information, but even more a medium for people's vicarious participation in social affairs; it gives them a sense of belonging, a sense of identity. This sense of identity amongst newspaper readers is carefully nurtured by the journalists, particularly of the more popular papers, when they address themselves personally to the reader or give the impression that they speak to him, representing the opinions and attitudes of Mr. Everyman. But while men can relate in some small measure to the world by means of their work, business or political allegiance, women are more isolated. The individual woman, even when she is in employment, has less contact with the world and its affairs and little corporate consciousness. Further, the rites and rituals, the values and duties which she was taught to observe in the past have disintegrated in the last hundred years, and the image of femininity previously upheld and communicated by cultural and religious traditions, has become unacceptable. Women's journals have stepped into the cultural void and provide her with a sense of self-recognition and a keyhole view of the big world outside – the world of men.

6. Women's Journals

The astonishing growth of women's journals is one of the social and cultural phenomena of our times. There are about thirty-seven women's journals on the market in England, varying in circulation from about three million (*Woman*) down to thirty-two thousand (*Harpers & Queen*). These figures are for 1969 and exclude sex or pornographic literature angled towards the female reader. This huge expansion since the Second World War has made women's magazines an important mass-communication medium far exceeding in number and variety every other type of journal except the major national newspapers. It is astonishing that in view of their great economic and social influence no sociological study of these journals has been made apart from a recent book by Cynthia L. White. I shall give a brief review of these journals not for the purpose of a sociological study but to show how the image of women has been affected by the recent changes in sexual expectations.

We shall see that on the one hand these journals, in varying degree, according to the class and intelligence of the reader to whom they are addressed, reflect modern sexual trends and, at the same time, manage to uphold many of the old certainties in order to reassure women who may be disturbed or confused by the conflicting demands of sexual modernism. We shall also glance at the trends in advertising and their exploitation of the new sex market.

The audience of the mass media expect to be sold goods and recipes for living. Readers want to be shown the commodities that make for good living and the images upon which they can model themselves and can identify with, and as a result emerge homogenised and stereotyped. While this has been widely deplored it is one of the attractions for the reader: they are freed from having to reflect upon themselves as individuals and can see themselves as belonging to the great community from which they are isolated in their actual lives.

Harpers & Queen, for instance, can be considered mainly as a magazine for the woman of the upper classes. The market to which she is introduced by advertising is very much in the upper price bracket. Only the money available to the readers of *Harpers & Queen* will buy the goods advertised in it.

The changes of sexual mores which are taking place in the world are duly acknowledged. A number of quite intelligent articles appear to keep the readers up to date, but all these articles show a sophisticated, benevolent interest, without considering any of the personal problems and conflicts upon which other women's journals reflect. The best articles are intelligent teasers, steering well away from betraying any serious commitment or conflict.

The sexual attractions of well-bred women are illustrated in romantic stories that often portray sexual adventures from the point of view of the male, quite frankly dealing with her desirability and the problems he encounters in her pursuit. The thing is not so much to experience the sexual revolution as a problem or as a liberation but to show that one can take it without a murmur; without flinching and with masterful good humour. There are fairly regular articles by Stephen Spender, among others, dealing with pornography, which, while not demanding of the reader any strong commitment, one way or another, inform and enlighten amusingly.

The woman of the world takes the revolution under her wing and patronises it. By adopting the sexual revolution she infuses taste and flair into it, she sees it as her duty to act as a civilising agent upon new cultural trends which, if entirely left in the hands of 'ordinary' people, would become barbaric. To harmonise new cultural developments, neither to be shocked nor alienated but to absorb them and give the impression that they can be enjoyed by those who know how to live, that is the aspiration of the woman of the British ruling class as reflected in this journal.

A little down the social scale we find *Vogue* magazine which, while being a trend-setter of the glamorous image of smartness and of elegance, appeals to a much wider range of women. It is a widely-read magazine for inspiration on what to buy and appeals to the middle-class, fashion-conscious woman. It illustrates how to dress smartly and fashionably without assuming that there are unlimited funds available: "Have you more fashion consciousness than money right now? You still have an eye to the international scene and top fashions." The fashions are more daring, more colourful and there is less emphasis upon restraint in the service of elegance. It acts very much as a high-class shop window where images of feminine glamour are displayed with the exciting personalities of the fashion and entertainment world as décor, and occasional illustrations from the world of science and art round off the window display. The sexual revolution here manifests itself essentially in the projection of the woman as a person who intends to participate in the world without in the least giving up her femininity and glamour. The sexual or emotional problems of women are not introduced into this journal.

In 1965 Dr. Ernest Dichter, then President of the Institute of Motivation Research, was commissioned to prepare a report on *Woman's Own*, "to assess its performance in relationship to the requirements of women readers at present and the possible requirements of the future." In his report Dichter pointed to changes concerning the needs, problems, goals, tastes and self-images of English women due to a wider and better education, exposure to mass media such as TV, affluence and the growth of women's employment, particularly after marriage. There is, he said, an inexorable movement towards greater independence, responsibility and social mobility for women bringing with it new interests and activities, wider social experience and cultural awareness.[1]

In these changes Dichter saw far-reaching implications for women's journals, such as the need for a more realistic approach, a wider range of features related to the broadening horizons of women's lives, improvements in format and type and art-work to bring them into line with modern tastes, and the acquisition of a specific character and a stated purpose with which groups of readers could identify. He concluded his report with a 51-point plan to bring *Woman's Own* into line with the changing requirements of contemporary women.

Though it was carried out specifically for *Woman's Own*, the general findings of Dichter's report were accepted by the International Publishing Corporation's group of women's magazines.[2] A new generation of younger editors was given the task of redefining the whole concept of publishing for women. A new editorial director was installed and it was his task to translate Dichter's suggestions into editorial policies. He and his colleagues set out to tackle issues like the morality of living on hire-purchase, explaining how supermarkets work, taking a deep look at the birth pill and all its implications: "It meant the breaking of a lot of taboos about what can be discussed and the manner in which they can be discussed in women's magazines ... the sexual experiences of women and men, sexual impotence, 'the other woman' – the kind of things which up till now had been only dealt with as brief footnotes to readers' letters in the old-style agony columns." As the new editorial director said: "The idea that a woman's magazine has to place a genteel filter between the subject and its reader must be hopelessly out of date at a time when any other medium can open up any issue for adult discussion."

It is as if men had discovered that they no longer have to select carefully what their women should read and present it to them in a manner suited to their limited understanding and their modesty, and that they could allow women to read the things which previously had been intended only for the male intelligence.

The new theories on women's magazines resulted in the launching of a new publication proclaiming itself to be "the new magazine for the new kind of woman." The magazine that was to cater for the new kind of woman, "the thinking female", was *Nova*: "The attitude group to which this magazine relates is characterised by the woman who 'could be 28 or 38, single with a job or married with children (and perhaps a job too), a girl with a university degree or a girl who never took school seriously. The social permutations are endless. What remains constant is that our new kind of woman has a wide range of interests, an enquiring mind and an independent outlook.' "[3] At least this is what many women would now like to be and this image is projected in the new journal.

While *Nova* is meant to appeal to the "new intelligent woman" this does not mean that it ignores the more traditional feminine interests. For all the modernity and intelligence of the women who are supposed to read this new journal there is a high proportion of ads which are identical with those found in traditional journals. The emphasis in those ads is upon the youngish educated woman who shows an interest in the world outside. Inevitably her image is rather middle-class which in this country goes with being educated. While there are no features on investment as in *Harpers* there are building society ads because the reader is assumed to be both practical and knowledgeable and able to look after her own financial interests. The intellectual content is not as in the traditional woman's magazine limited roughly to 5% – 10% of reading matter, but forms a substantial part of the journal; it is not confined to presenting reflections about the world by selecting a woman in the public eye and using her personal view as an entrée to political or social problems. *Nova* does not consider this to be necessary, and assumes that its public can read and understand the real problems of the world. In one issue there was an article on the colour problem at Brixton, one on I.Q. tests by Ruth Inglis and one on monogamy in which Sally Vincent probes the one-for-one system. This article, while expressing the modern cynicism towards the institution of marriage, nevertheless concludes that the factors in its favour outweigh any considerations against it:

> "Women's Lib tell us we've bred a whore in every home and every domestic law in the land seems to protect this state of affairs. 'Marriage', said Brigid Brophy, 'is the price men pay for sexual intercourse and sexual intercourse the price women pay for marriage.' She was wrong. Men pay far, far more than marriage for their first fine careless rapture. And they go on paying whether they like it or not. Even fifth-form harpies are sure of that ...
> Since monogamy grew from economic causes, might it not fade away in its present form when those causes cease to exist? As women look upon themselves as beings capable of earning their own livings, instead of as creatures searching for someone with external genitalia to earn it for

them, the sort of prostitution complex that goes with the old idea of a woman's place will die. Monogamy then might stand a chance of becoming a reality and the concept of everyone's other half something more than a myth."

In the same issue there is also an article on faith-healing and evangelism and a feature on "boobs" from every angle. The modern girl talks in a joking, deprecating way about her "boobs" rather than breasts. This is aimed at titivating male readers as well as giving a useful survey for women on the various methods of increasing bust size and improving its firmness. There was also an extraordinary feature "presenting a lot of useful facts about men, as ammunition for every argument" – a look at the differences between men and women in the form of an assortment of facts gathered from social and statistical surveys, some giving what appear to be totally irrelevant and possibly amusing information, others quite interesting. To quote a few of these snippets of information:

"According to the latest figures men are distinctly more sickly than women, in some areas dramatically more frail."

"According to Masters and Johnson there is no relation between the size of a man's skeletal framework and that of his external genitalia. Among Masters and Johnson's study subjects, the man with the longest penis is only 5ft. 7in. tall ... On average a man's brain is 4 oz. heavier than a woman's, which is nothing to gloat over or get upset about since Neanderthal man's brain was much bigger than that of modern man ... "

"In his book, *The Body,* Anthony Smith says that the female has 4%–5% quantitative superiority in genetic (chromosal) material than man. He also points out that married men are mentally and physically healthier than single men ... Men experience higher blood pressure when making love than women do ... The number of men found guilty of rape in 1970 was 304; curiously, one woman was! Of the 2,055 persons summoned in 1971 for thefts of pedal bicycles only 48 were women."

Here, and in a number of other articles, we can see the development from the goals outlined in the early formulation of editorial policy of *Nova* towards a trend of competitiveness with the male. The sexual revolution which in the early sixties emphasised the personal and sexual equality of women has shifted towards a preoccupation with the new woman's need to hold her own against man, to prove that she is as good as he is, or better; able to think and converse freely about sexual matters, including the sexuality of the male. The introduction of risqué subjects in a bland and matter-of-fact way is characteristic of this new trend where the woman has to emulate man's sexual freedom and cease being frightened or coy about his sexuality. As we shall see, the overt discussion about men's penises, previously the most secret of female preoccupations and fantasies is meant to show that the modern woman is no longer intimidated by man.

In another issue, there is an 'advanced' article by Charlotte Hopson: 'How Much Togetherness Can A Marriage Stand?' It questions the traditional mystique of the marital virtue of togetherness "when the husband and wife must always appear together as a couple, share the same friends ... always share vacations ... put their money in a conjugal financial pot, and must never feel attraction to anyone else of the opposite sex." The article goes on to reflect that:

> "The tragedy of this pattern of 'togetherness' is that each partner's need for a variety of relationships may be stifled. This threatens the growth of the partners and their marriage. It also places impossible pressures on an individual who feels he must somehow act as a substitute for the wide circle of friends who are now forbidden fruit to his mate. It should be no slight on a person to discover that he cannot provide the satisfactions that a number of friends once offered his partner.
>
> This Siamese-twin existence makes it impossible for two people to establish separate identities. Why separate identities anyway? Because if one partner exists at the expense of the other, both partners lose out. They lose the opportunity to develop through the relationship rather than in spite of it ... "

Nova projects an image of the modern woman who takes pride in having liberated herself from many taboos concerning the relationship between the sexes, who blandly knows about men and enters into relationships with them on a footing of personal equality and independence. However, she safeguards the institution of marriage by expressing her spontaneity and her intelligence within it. The modern emancipated woman claims the right to sexual stimulation, and the more 'advanced' a woman's journal intends to be, the more must it feel free to satisfy this need in an open and uninhibited manner.

Cosmopolitan, the woman's journal which was founded in 1971, endeavours to express the new trend where *Nova* stops short. It goes a lot further in the publication of really 'daring' sexual features, showing a frankness in writing and graphic detail almost as great as that of *Forum* but in the traditional woman's magazine form. Problems of sexual relationships are more deliberately featured and *Cosmopolitan* goes out to satisfy the modern woman's demand to be informed about her sexual functions. The topic of sexual gratification of women, having been brought out of the lumber-room of secret fantasies and intellectual confusion, demands clarification. What has been secret and hidden in the past, even from women's own consciousness, is to be revealed, and the world is to discover the true sexual nature of woman, her demands and her desires. What Freud, Stekel, Helene Deutsch and Reich discussed in their clinical papers, *Cosmopolitan* is to present to the great public in a handsome format and with glossy illustrations.

Just as fashion has freed women's legs and breasts from the cover of secrecy so she no longer needs to hide her emotions and her sexual feelings. The new woman who claims her place in the world as an equal to men, demands an equal right to discuss uninhibitedly and articulately all the matters pertaining to sex previously considered taboo or unseemly. Articles intended to promote women's understanding of their sexuality and to tell them how to obtain full gratification feature largely in every issue. Articles like 'Any Woman Can' (that is to say any woman can experience the greatest of all pleasures, namely sexual fulfilment), 'One Man Is Not Enough', just to mention a few, go much further and are much more open in giving sexual information than can be found in other women's journals.

6. WOMEN'S JOURNALS

Besides articles on the nature of female sexuality and its problems there are two other types of article of interest to us: those showing women how they can become sexually exciting and fascinating – a sort of introduction to sexual etiquette – and others dealing with exciting men, either in the form of articles about their lives and loves and what makes them tick, or photographs of male nudes. These photographs of men are fairly restrained and not blatant, although one husband of a celebrated 'modern' woman appeared in a full-frontal photograph with his penis clearly shown.

Some of the articles in this journal, which claims to be and probably is the most advanced of women's journals to date but does not come into the category of pornography, are:

'Female Orgasm – What It Is And What It Is Not', from the book *Female Sexuality* by Sandra McDermott.

This book tries to convey in an explicit and intelligent manner the woman's experience of orgasm. The author briefly mentions the theories of Freud and Reich on orgasm and considers them verified in the experiments of Masters and Johnson. She also discusses the new obsession with female orgasm as one of the less beneficial results of the sexual emancipation of women. She then interviews a number of women asking them to describe an orgasm in order to convey to the reader what an orgastic experience feels like.

Another article concerned with the sexual role of the single woman is entitled: 'All You Need To Know For A More Adventurous Love Life', from a recent book by Ruth Dickson.[4]

This is quite a serious article and informative. It takes for granted the right to sexual fulfilment of women, whether single or married, and stresses the point that the marriage certificate cannot keep two people happy, that much more than this is required, probably the most important of which is leading an active and exciting sex life, and it is up to the single girl to understand this and learn how to acquire the skills and knowledge needed. The author strongly criticises the taboos which have stood in the way of a woman's fulfilment and advises the reader how to liberate herself from these taboos and how to go about acquiring an enlightened attitude to sex. The article enjoins women to learn about male and female anatomy, as well as about orgasm, in order to overcome the abysmal ignorance which is inculcated in our culture, particularly in women, and causes all kinds of irrational fears. She then discusses the relationship between love and sexuality and agrees that sexual intercourse with the person one loves is the ideal. But she puts in this proviso:

> "But don't for a minute think you can't have a good, wholesome sex life without it. You can have a wonderful time with men you just like. Once you've got over the notion that you can't be a Total Woman unless you have One Right Man, you'll find innumerable opportunities for friendly sexual relationships." [5]

She proposes a number of games to facilitate sexual happiness. One of the games she suggests is that the two partners change their sex roles and play-act the attitude and state of mind of the other.

The articles concerned with sexual etiquette feature women who are sexually attractive and successful. The reader can learn from them how to become desirable, model herself upon them and vicariously experience their rich and varied lives. They are the new female totem figures to which the modern woman aspires.

In an article entitled 'These Women Are Dangerous' (May 1972), Douglas Keay called on four of these ladies and interviewed them.

The article is angled to introduce these women to the readers as dangerous to them insofar as they have that something which makes them very attractive to men and, as such, dangerous to other women. Their very danger, as it were, is an implied token of their feminine power.

> "In every woman's life there are 'other women', often strangers, who have only to appear at a party, on television, at the back-door and within a second of their smiling, crossing a leg, asking for the loan of a loaf, the warning signals

go off like a thousand burglar-alarms – 'Help!' and 'Keep away from my man!' and 'How do you do it?' – all spring to mind at once and are met with a pale and innocent look that fools no one. These women (and we can all think of half-a-dozen at least) are often beautiful, frequently are not particularly young and their marriages are sometimes happy. These are the women that men look out for and women have to watch out for."

Besides learning how to be sexually attractive from the acknowledged mistresses in the art, the reader of *Cosmopolitan* is also given more direct instructions through articles that teach her how to acquire 'A Sexy Shape Through Basic Yoga Exercises', 'Rock Dance Away To A Sexy Figure' and others designed, not as in the past, to acquire a healthy and shapely figure but a sexy figure. The etiquette of sexual behaviour is also catered for by instructive articles, such as 'How To Be A Perfect New Girl In The Office', 'How To Be Your Own Best Friend', 'How You Can Use Your Star Sign To Become More Fascinating'.

If, after all these introductions to the world of the sexually liberated woman and the instructions on how to become one, the reader still has problems, there are the services of a psychoanalyst available without extra cost. A feature 'On the couch' by Renatus Hartogs, MD, PhD, appears in every issue and answers and discusses readers' sexual problems.

Among the third type of features, i.e. those dedicated to presenting fascinating and exciting men, we find an article entitled: 'Are These The World's Most Exciting Men?' It shows photographs and gives short descriptions of 33 varied types of men, mostly from the entertainment and sporting world "to start you arguing". This shows the new trend or, one might call it, revolution, which encourages women to regard men as sex objects in an open and conscious manner as it was hitherto the prerogative of men to consider women. There is a nude photograph of one of these desirable objects of women's fancy together with a horse.

There is another article, 'Bare Flesh Is Big Business – Male Models Uncovered', with full-page pictures in colour of five nude men in various poses of masculinity:

"Bare female flesh, of course, has been big business for years. Any girl with the face, the figure, the inclination and a certain *je ne sais quoi* can make big money by learning to take her clothes off in a suitably titillating fashion. In fact the big-time nude models of today, like beautiful Vivien Neves, are in some ways equivalent to the cocottes of the nineteenth century. The difference is that instead of giving themselves for real to a few men in exchange for money and sparklers, these girls offer the two-dimensional image of their bodies as dream substitutes for millions of men ... Male modelling has until recently been slightly suspect as a career and men seem to have a very strong built-in resistance to revealing themselves in public. But at last there are joyful signs of a breakthrough ... "[6]

The courtesan in the shop window of colour magazines, who does not have to give herself to her clients, who does not even see or know any of her million admirers, is now complemented by males as depersonalised sexual commodities to celebrate the equality between the sexes. Women too can now gaze at sex objects behind the plate-glass window. To substitute for the complete lack of any personal contact between client and the male or female courtesan, little potted biographies and descriptions of their personalities are provided, so that the two-dimensional picture behind the window can acquire a modicum of the third dimension, namely personal relationship.

We can see that *Cosmopolitan* has become increasingly explicit in its articles dealing with female sexuality, giving information about aspects of a woman's life which are important to her well-being and self-fulfilment. It eschews hypocrisy and modesty and in doing so intends to project an image of its readers as intelligent and open-minded women, prepared to think and to cope with problems. Indeed, this journal along with *Nova* cultivates a new public among women who may be termed the female meritocracy. Although most of these women are middle class, they rely on education and ability to claim their place in society; they would wish to succeed by dint of ability and intelligence rather than privilege, either of birth or marriage, unlike

6. WOMEN'S JOURNALS

the readers of journals like *Harpers & Queen* for instance, which appeal to privilege of birth and marriage and are quite openly conservative in outlook. The female meritocrat, being in opposition to the male-dominated establishment, tends to be vaguely liberal. (The consciously left-wing woman is restrained from being a regular reader of journals like *Cosmopolitan* because of its glossy consumer-orientated outlook.) The critique of the established system, however, extends only to the restraints it has placed upon women's participation in it. The 'modern woman' does not wish to overthrow the establishment but to participate in it.

When we turn to the mass circulation journals like *Woman* we encounter a paradox. This journal is read mostly by working-class and lower middle-class women but is in respect to sexual mores quite conservative. The lower one goes in the social scale the more one encounters acquiescence to patriarchal morality. (We must make a proviso here with regard to the very young members of the working-class.) These journals appeal to married women, housewives who, having accepted the situation of marriage, are concerned with making it work and do not wish to question the foundations and framework of their existence. Of course they wish to improve their appearance, they are fascinated by beautiful women and by interesting men, but they rely on traditional symbols of vicarious satisfaction, i.e. film stars, tycoons and royalty. Responsibility for the home and the ability to cope with deprivations, sickness, children's problems are deep-seated virtues among working-class women. They cannot afford the sophistications and doubts of their better educated and more ambitious sisters. How to be a good wife and keep one's self-respect as a married woman, how to make oneself more attractive and improve one's ability as a cook, how to provide cheap and attractive clothing for oneself and one's children, how to cope with husband and children – these are the fundamental issues that occupy the minds of the great majority of women. "Even film stars, even the Queen," they are told, "have responsibilities to the home and family, like yourselves."

Of course, idealism and rebellion against the established order is perfectly all right while one is young, but when you settle down to the real job of living, you learn how to appreciate the little things, to accept responsibilities and to care for your family. Of course, every mother comes across the new permissiveness among the young, and it is difficult to know where to draw the line. Children are exposed to fads and fantasies and they are impressionable, so the new sexual permissiveness and the fad of women's liberation affects the attitudes of young girls. (There is no need to worry too much about the boys in this respect because they have always been unruly and that has been more or less accepted.) A mother who cares for her children must seek to understand and not merely condemn.

To show some understanding for the young, and not to be entirely ignorant about the new fashions, to uphold traditional values and, at the same time, to show fairness and a measure of tolerance has been, and still is, the overriding virtue of the hard-working housewife and mother. As to the supposed equality between the sexes: of course, men are sexually more restless than women, they always had certain social advantages, but that is nothing new; after all they are the providers and the family depends upon them, and often they have to struggle hard enough in all conscience to make ends meet. A woman who knows about men understands that they are subjected to all sorts of pressure in their work and in the world outside and their lives are not all roses. And when a man comes home in the evening, he wants a little comfort and relaxation, otherwise he soon gets fed up. It is all very well for 'them', who don't have to struggle for a living, who have all sorts of fancy notions, in fact, half the time they are so bored they don't know what to do with themselves, so they get discontented and dream up all sorts of new problems. Maybe a bit more equality, a few more opportunities for women, a bit of help occasionally in the home, and a bit more appreciation would not come amiss. Equal pay for women and equal opportunities to go into the best jobs if they have the talent for it, perhaps the right to experiment a little sexually before marriage, may be good things, but one can go too far and cause more harm than good. After all, women do have so many more opportunities now than ever before and if, sometimes, people fall in love and have children outside marriage, it is no longer such a terrible sin as it was a generation ago. We have grown more tolerant, but marriage

6. WOMEN'S JOURNALS

is marriage, and a woman has to look after her children and her husband if he supports the family, and that is the rule that has gone on for centuries. The alternative would be confusion and hardship for everybody. Some women overdo this equality business, they go too far.

We must realise that among the readers of a mass-circulation journal like *Woman* the majority are still under the influence of the economics of scarcity, i.e. they have to work hard in order to satisfy their needs whether they be basic, like paying the rent and providing enough food for the family, or whether they include the demands of the consumer society like television, radio, motor cars, home decoration to keep up with the Joneses, and the annual holiday abroad. These women have been taught to be grateful for the rewards of hard work, and frugality and self-denial are still admirable qualities. Self-denial relates not merely to material things but also to emotional and sexual needs, but this is compensated for by a sense of approval for doing one's duty, keeping the family together, feeding and caring for them, keeping a nice home, serving the country and seeing to it that the men of the family are sent out into the world well fed, contented and secure. The rewards of marital fidelity are fundamentally self-evident and need not be questioned. Secret longings and fantasies can be satisfied through romantic stories and vicarious experiences.

The sexual revolution impinges upon these women only peripherally, i.e. by a certain worry or confusion about the attitudes of their children and by a little more daringness of the romances they read; they can see it in the more tolerant attitudes in the letter columns of their journals and in more open-minded correspondence concerning V.D. and birth control. Their journals do not discuss the actual sexual needs of women in an overt, unsublimated manner. In a letter to *Woman* a wife suffering from "intimate" boredom is told not to look outside marriage, but to understand her husband and arouse him. While *Woman* tries to widen the scope of its interests, one of its editors has remarked: "The criterion of what the magazine can include is still whether or not it is accepted by the population at large. If *Woman* can talk about abortion, the sex pill, even sex from a man's point of view, this reflects the acceptance of a wider view among the large masses of the population and a desire to be aware of new trends, but the way it can write about these matters is determined by the limits which the average woman sets to changes she can accept."

Woman's Own is Newnes' counterpart to Odhams' *Woman*. Its image is similar to that of *Woman* even though it makes occasional excursions into being explicit about sex. Its age image is also a little on the younger side.

Woman's Own was founded in 1932 for women in charge of small homes, and the editorial section at that time offered special domestic articles, cooking features, personal pages, sensible beauty advice, fashion (to make at home), baby-care, knitting and needlework, and help with personal problems and worries, tense human and true-to-life stories. The journal has broadly kept to these policies and although the true human stories are often quite unlifelike, personal problems include some advice on sex, while nothing that could be disturbing to traditional morality is discussed.

Lest we have gained the impression that a discussion of sex matters is something very new, let us remember that in the early 1930s a writer in *Good Housekeeping* reflected on the impact of Freud's writings upon the conspiracy of silence concerning the sexuality of women:

> "Freud, whether right or wrong, did succeed in convincing women that they had sex desires, and that these desires were not wicked; that to repress them was as difficult and dangerous to women as to men and that they need no longer pretend that all they wanted was at most motherhood, when it was quite as natural for them to want loverhood. This has been an astounding change ... Even to know what marriage meant was formerly regarded as unsuitable in women, and to want to know, indecent ... The result of such a violent fracture has been bad as well as good. Instead of the terrifying repression of the old maid, we have the complete repudiation of any kind of self-control as a danger to her sanity or, at least, to the normal and free development of her age. It was perhaps an inevitable reaction – from the

6. WOMEN'S JOURNALS

false belief that the physical side of marriage meant nothing to a woman to the obsession with sex which has now prevailed for some years."

With the exception of educated and progressive women who in the 1920s welcomed Freud's ideas with alacrity, the great majority of women in this country remained under the domination of 'respectability' and the conspiracy of silence. It was different in the countries of Europe which underwent a socialist revolution after the First World War. The socialist revolutions, while relatively short-lived and mostly abortive, nevertheless opened up the shutters imposed by the old regimes, encouraged rebellion against the taboos (associated with feudal and bourgeois establishments) and a certain openness of mind and freedom for women. Indeed, equality for women was among the first items on the agenda of any self-respecting revolutionary movement. We know what happened to the revolutions in Europe, we know about the reactionary counterblast of Hitler and the degeneration of socialist morality under Stalin, but the overthrow of the old regimes weakened the old respectabilities and gave European women a certain sophistication in matters of sex lacking in those countries which did not experience social revolutions.

It is evident that since the Second World War this country is trying to catch up in its acceptance of the sexuality of women, but it is important to notice that this does not in any way affect the political and moral attitudes of the majority which continues to be traditionalistic. The social and moral changes of the last thirty years has affected 'the silent majority' only peripherally. For them the social structure has not changed very much, their consciousness of social and moral transformation is clouded by the old loyalties and values, despite some loosening up of taboos and compulsions.

It is different with the young, the children of the 'silent majority'. If we consider the journals catering for the teenage girls of the working and lower middle-classes, we can see a much greater impact of the new social and sexual outlook. The earlier maturation of girls and their resentment towards paternal and social restrictions makes them critical of the *status quo,* and their search for an alternative identity drives them to embrace the new morality.

The magazine *She* which blazed the trail of the new female image way back in 1955 (some ten years before *Nova),* while not pretending to the intellectual image of *Nova,* caters for the young women of a fairly wide social and educational range. We can see in its readers the daughters of the women who read magazines like *Woman* and *Woman's Own* and who, while not necessarily aspiring towards the managerial or professional class, as those of *Nova* or *Cosmopolitan* do, have acquired a certain freedom of mind and independence. It is less ambitious and determined in its modernity than *Nova* and we notice a light-hearted atmosphere, a sense of amusement at the new scene and a capacity to enjoy it. *She* caters not so much for the teenage girls but for the woman who is consciously young, usually in her twenties and who deliberately turns away from the life-style of her mother. There is an article in a recent issue, entitled 'The Man Who Came In With The Coal', telling the tale of a woman of thirty-seven who is happily married but who suddenly realises that she has never had another man besides her husband and becomes curious as to whether she is missing anything. Not that she has any fault to find with her husband's sexual powers, but she wants to know whether he was average or whether other men were better at it, or worse. So she thought she had better find out before it is too late. She eventually made it with a young and beautiful coalman who was most exciting and satisfactory as a lover:

> "I'd never believed that women can't have a sexual relationship without becoming emotionally involved. Of course they can. That's just a myth created by men to preserve the double standard. And the Pill of course has removed any fear of pregnancy. We both had a marvellous time. We made love a lot, and we laughed a lot and we liked each other but no more than that.
>
> All good things come to an end and in time the regular coalman returned, so John and I had a final session and a final beer and said good-bye.
>
> I doubt whether I shall ever see him again and I don't

know that I really want to. In a way it was a relief to be able to tell the truth about my movements. Having a lover is so complicated it's almost too much trouble. Certainly it was great fun while it lasted and I know now that my husband's performance in bed is excellent; that I am still sexually attractive and that sex without love is good clean fun but sex with love is an experience on a different plane altogether. All in all, it was a very worthwhile experiment. Better than tranquillisers any day." [7]

While being fairly explicit in a quasi D. H. Lawrence manner, it emphasises the good-natured amusement of the relationship, its pleasure without too much involvement, and the superiority of a sexual relationship with the loved husband. But it also emphasises the new freedom from guilt and the woman's right for a bit of experimentation. The same issue features an article about a sex-dialling service in New York where people can receive information concerning sex problems which they are too inhibited to discuss with anyone they know. This article mentions, *en passant,* how some men masturbate when they talk to the woman counsellor on the telephone and her matter-of-fact attitude when she realises this.

The almost inevitable exercises to gain a more sexy body have their place in this journal, and one feature entitled 'Sex-ercises' instructs how to get the body into beautiful condition for living as well as loving. Sexual lovemaking, it claims, is enjoyed most by those who have trained the muscles which specifically have to do with sexual performance. It deals quite sensibly with the importance of breathing, pointing to the breathing restrictions experienced by anxious and inhibited people.

If we now compare the circulation figures of the traditional journals, in which the changes in sexual attitudes have only had a peripheral impact, with those journals which adopt a deliberately progressive attitude, then we gain a fair impression of the extent to which the sexual revolution has influenced grown-up women in this country.

Woman has a circulation of approximately three million, *Woman's Own* about two million and *Woman's Weekly,* which is also a traditional journal, a circulation of approximately one and a half million. While these three journals are bought by about six and a half million women, the magazines *Nova, Cosmopolitan* and *She* together have a circulation of something like 700,000 copies. It is true that the latter are monthlies and more expensive than the first-mentioned, but nevertheless the 'modern' magazines have a circulation of slightly more than one-tenth of the 'traditional' magazines. We must, of course, bear in mind that the modern magazines are read by the more ambitious and articulate women who are likely to set the trend in social values and who have a larger influence upon public thinking than their numbers imply. Even so, it is as well to realise that they are very much in the minority and traditionalism, albeit a somewhat more permissive traditionalism, is still a dominating force.

Let us now turn to the journals which cater for female teenagers who earn their own living, have a great sense of belonging to the new generation, claim to be in the know and to be sexually confident and liberated, who have their own world of fashions, and a new type of relationship with boys based upon equality and no old-fashioned hang-ups, thank you! At least, that is the image they like to have of themselves. As these girls earn, relatively speaking, a good income, they have money to spend and they spend it, and the advertisers are only too aware of this. They are the teenage daughters of the readers of *Woman, Woman's Own* and *Woman's Weekly,* the modern working girl, conscious of her early maturity and her membership of a generation with its own alternative image.

In the journals catering for them there is, as in *She,* an atmosphere which is light-hearted and youthfully sophisticated with a fair amount of banter and flippancy while, at the same time, there is a degree of serious curiosity concerning those things which her mother would regard as only of interest to men.

The magazines that cater for these girls are conscious of their spending power, as is the fashion trade that since the late '50s has made a powerful bid for this new market, switching from the quality garments required by older women to the mass-production of fashions for the younger generation. As Cynthia L. White has remarked, "The high fashion demands of teenagers have trans-

6. WOMEN'S JOURNALS

formed the rag trade and the journals associated with fashion." The young female wage-earner, in whose budget food occupies a very small place, may have as much as £12–£15 a week to spend on clothes, cosmetics and hairdressing. The wise men of the garment industry have learned to cash in on the new trend even to the extent of becoming the trend-setters for the young, from the psychedelic fashions of the sixties, and the freedom of girls' limbs in mini dresses, to the militaristic look and now the unisex look, which helps girls to affirm their sexual equality. By trying to look like boyish hoodlums, tramps or drug addicts, they show their disdain for traditional expectations of femininity.

The magazine *Honey,* which started in 1961, was originally a fashion journal and soon turned its attention almost exclusively to the enormously expanding teenage market. Its policy was to appeal to the better-income teenage girls "who are everything that is young, gay and going-far." These are girls with several 'O' levels, possibly some 'A' levels, earning perhaps £15–£20 per week at that time, which would now be considerably more. While the journal's prime policy is to stimulate interest in fashion, it also includes general features of interest to the educated young girl. These girls proselytise the new freedom for women, not through books, religion or political allegiances, but through personal behaviour and appearance.

The new life-style and the new identity must be shown in their appearance, ideas need not be argued in books or on the platform or even in discussion, but are communicated by the way girls look. In order to be revolutionary you have to look like a revolutionary, the pictorial ideology, the strip-cartoon philosophy, is the order of the day when people can instantly see what you stand for. It is not merely beauty or attractiveness in the old sense that concerns the youngsters but the visual communication of a life-style. And the fashion industry can provide the costumes, the photographers and designers provide the decor, the gramophone and recording industries the sound and the music, the film industry the animation and the chorus. The chemical industry is there to enhance and regulate your body smells by a variety of deodorants; it can improve your skin, your hair, your teeth, your eyes, your lips, give you a sun-tan, soften you, smooth you, cleanse you and hygienise you. Deodorant sprays for sexual freshness liberate you from any embarrassment caused by vaginal discharge, takes care of the inner and outer vaginal areas, keeping you confident all day.

If you have any fears of old age encroaching upon you once you push twenty, there is a whole battery of creams and potions which guarantee to rejuvenate you and maintain that teenage look. For after all, we are what we appear and if we are sophisticated and take advantage of all the new aids for health and well-being, vitamin pills, health foods and promoters of internal cleanliness, then we are as good as we feel. If, after all these things, that teenage *joie de vivre*, that scintillating sense of well-being and happiness sometimes eludes us, then the establishment will provide us with the necessary mood promoters.

So much for the advertisers and the dreams they purvey to young people, who need these dreams to fortify their self-image and who have the money to purchase them. The religion of the consumer society is, of course, not restricted to the teenagers, but it finds here its most lucrative and most promising worshippers. But to do them justice, we can admit that the youngsters have a mind of their own, they are, despite all appearances and the efforts of the image industry, concerned about things and want to know all about the world. If you wish to engage in the old-fashioned pastime of reading books, if you can't help being intelligent then *Honey* can give you some considered advice to prevent you from wasting your time on the wrong books, particularly if you go on holiday:

> "No native leaves these shores without a goodly stock of tales of murder, sex and romance. Most people don't read more than a few thousand words of books from one month to the next but in transit and abroad, away from work and television, we go at the printed page like the scholars of old ... Only perverts read good books on holidays, normal people go for something 'lighter.' Sadism, cannibalism, torture, that kind of thing. Books that bring blood to your eyeballs. Very nice too ... One slow, weighty book, with not so

much as a pant of lust in the first fifty pages would be enough to undo a thousand package tours. Imagine the yelps of frustration that would go up from the shores of Spain as sunbathers discovered that the morning's reading hadn't rendered one rape or the arrival of an other-worldly monster. If innocence was what we wanted we'd take a prayer book." [8]

Besides the usual romance stories, kept in a cool and amusing vein, there are occasional serious and sensible articles in *Honey* and in other teenage magazines, showing a vein of sincerity and genuine interest among young girls who, despite all their rebellious play-acting (or is it because of it, having allowed them a certain amount of aggressive catharsis?) feel sincere sympathy towards human problems which their more 'well-adjusted' elders often ignore.

The vein of sincerity is manifest in the magazine *Look Now* which caters for a younger teenage public. Its ads are more limited in scope and while it is exceedingly well produced in the modern manner, is less glossy.

There are many features strong on concern for the state of the world. One entitled 'Caring Is Sharing' points to several things the young girl can do to help the homeless, the old and the sick. An article entitled 'Who Cares' lists a number of organisations a young girl can join to do her bit to improve the world: Save the Children Fund, Oxfam, Shelter, the NSPCC, the National Society for Open Air, The Pure Air Society, The Pure Rivers Society, The Society for the Promotion of Nature Reserves, etc., etc. It assures its readers that "if you care, you are not alone – so do hundreds of thousands of people in the country. You can help and you can always write to us at *Look Now* for further information."

There is still plenty of room for advertisements of the kind mentioned earlier, for while the spending ability of these girls is limited, they will soon grow into money-earning young women and have to be cultivated.

The magazine *19* is similar to *Look Now* inasmuch as it also caters for the young teenager, but it is more deliberately modern or radical in outlook. It could be called the young girl's *Nova* and in parts is more intelligent and vivacious than *Nova* without being quite so outspoken about sex. One can see here the young girl being prepared to become the female meritocrat, a woman with personality, ability, and ideas, who can, if she really tries, make some impact upon the world, influence public opinion and government policy. There is a similar bland and ambitious atmosphere in this journal as we find in *Nova,* the same emphasis upon the woman as an active and responsible member of society on the side of progress, ready to assert herself against hypocrisy and old-fashioned humbug.

The stress here is upon the new generation which will be able to run the world much better than the older generation has managed, and women have to get ready to play a major part in it. While there is no attempt whatsoever at any social analysis, there is a concern with objectives to which young people can subscribe. In a recent issue there is also a sympathetic article on Lesbianism, and any girl wishing to obtain more information about it is invited to apply to Gay Liberation Front and other Lesbian organisations. What particularly struck me is the tone of women's liberation propaganda discernible in this article. Whole passages could be taken from the books of old campaigners like Shulamith Firestone and Kate Millett. The article also quotes the editress of *Sappho,* the Lesbian magazine: "I find that homosexual women are absolutely essential to the women's movement as a whole, because they are totally free of the economic structure based on the male: Lesbians are not property to be owned, neither do they subscribe to the nuclear family. I am very conscious of *Sappho's* commitment to women's liberation – we think of ourselves as women first, Lesbians second." [9]

There is no doubt that this magazine presents an image of the young girl who is concerned with the alternative society, who wants to overcome the hiatus of feminine inferiority by asserting female independence, equality and ability.

To round off this review of women's journals I have to mention *Petticoat* – another teenage magazine founded in 1966, having a circulation of about two hundred thousand.

Honey made a big hit with the late teens but the young teens were not catered for until the arrival of *Petticoat*. Created as a younger sister to *Honey*, *Petticoat* was geared to the fast growing, early teen fashion trade. The journal is directed to the less-educated young girls, mostly of the working-class and here we see again the same paradox as in *Woman* in that the lower one goes in the social scale, the less concern there is with ideological changes. It provides plenty of stories in a sentimental vein, and the new sexual equality and freedom is mostly reflected in its advertisements.

The more equal a girl is expected to be, the more exposed she feels and the more she will require the commodities which enhance her personality and give her confidence. The youth revolution and female emancipation has created a new and self-conscious market for the commodity pedlars. One cannot actually say that the youth revolution was initiated by the manufacturers but they certainly took it up and promoted it to the full. In capitalist consumer-orientated society, the social importance of a section of the population is measured by its purchasing power. Business is very concerned with social transformations which create a significant new class of purchasers – business is there to promote its aspirations and supply its needs. It will do more than that – it will adopt the emerging classes as its favourite customers, will anticipate their tastes and cultivate them. It is important for business to understand the psychological needs of its customers and the type of commodities they require in order to enhance their prestige in society. And while in the old days the flair and intuition of the entrepreneur enabled him to do this, nowadays big firms employ sociologists and psychologists to arrive at a correct estimate of the likely demands of new and growing markets. Whether they are publishers of women's journals or belong to the cosmetics and clothing industry (and, in any case, the three work in close conjunction), they provide the most scientific information on social trends available today. Women's journals, therefore, reflect the new aspirations and self-image of women of various ages and classes and their response to the sexual revolution.

To sum up, we can say that the sexual revolution is having a considerable impact upon educated women and has facilitated the creation of a self-conscious female meritocracy, and it is widely influencing young girls. Their sexual freedom and sense of equality is, without a doubt, greatly enhanced and their objectives in life transcend the traditional boundaries set to women. We have seen that the visual image of style and fashion is an important aspect of the new role they wish to play, and that they are exploited in this respect by the manufacturing and business establishments. It is they who provide the new image and women are almost completely dependent upon them. If we are to ask whether the new aspirations and the new self-image are genuine and have established a new psychological and spiritual freedom then doubt enters the mind in view of the fact that the revolution of the female image is consumer-orientated, and one gains the impression that besides the real advantages which come from the new permissiveness, its effect upon the social structure is minimal.

If you are obliged to *buy* all the props for your rebellion, if commerce provides you with the wherewithal of a new image, then your rebellion and your new image is bound to be a fashion and will be subject to changes of fashion. Ideas and expectations are, therefore, subjected to the rules of commerce; you recognise yourself through the commodity which you purchase, you consume modernity and in this respect you are yourself – from the point of view of commerce – a commodity. Your ideas and lifestyle become a market commodity and can be manipulated by business.

1. Dr. Ernest Dichter: *A Motivational Research Study on the British Woman in Today's Culture*.
2. Cynthia L. White: *Women's Magazines 1693–1968* (Michael Joseph, 1970).
3. *World Press News*, 1st March 1965.
4. Ruth Dickson (1972): 'Now You Have Got Me Here, What Are You Going To Do?'
5. *Cosmopolitan*: January 1973.
6. *Cosmopolitan*: May 1972.
7. *She*: January 1973.
8. *Honey*: July 1972: 'To the Beaches Where Bad Books Are Best', by David Robson.
9. *19 Magazine* (1973), *IPC* Magazines Ltd.

7. Pornography

Pornography has always existed in our culture and the business connected with the selling of pictures and pornographic literature has had its place in every large city. The traditional or hardcore pornography is therefore nothing new, and has nothing to do with the sexual revolution. Brothels and pornography have always gone together like the selling of illustrated brochures in museums.

A new trend observable in the last twenty years is in the popularisation of journals largely devoted to pornography, the enormous expansion in their numbers, and the image they project as respectable journals, fit to be read by all men who consider themselves young and progressive.

There is much discussion about the desirability of this pornographic proliferation, whether it should be permitted or restrained by law, whether it is harmful or beneficial. A polarisation of viewpoints has become manifest between those who welcome it as a sign of maturity in society, even as a therapeutic catharsis, and others who condemn it. Those who support the spreading of pornography for psychological and political reasons see in it the manifestation of the sexual liberation that will overcome the old taboos and fears upon which authoritarian society is based. Others see it as an undermining of morality and of civilised values. However, there are doubts in many people's minds and a sense of unease about the real significance of the spread of pornography.

The meaning of pornography is widely discussed in order to arrive at a workable definition of it for censorship purposes. This type of discussion does not provide an insight into the nature of pornography and its meaning for the human psyche and for the culture in which it flourishes.

Other interested parties in this debate are those engaged in the publication and distribution of pornography. The men who are in business are not concerned with psychological health or ethics; they are concerned with demand and profit. And of course the demand is there. If one deals with the pedlars of any other merchandise, one knows where one stands with them, and very often they are quite honest about their motivations even if they will do their bit of moralistic rationalisation. It is different, though, with the sexual commodity pedlars who claim to be devoted to the promotion of sexual liberation and happiness, combating the old taboos and repressions. However, they mistake opportunity for motivation. It is as if the brothel madam claimed to stand in the vanguard of sexual freedom whereas clearly she can only remain in business on the basis of her customers' frustration in a sex-negating world. The trouble is that the modern customers of pornography mistake the availability of it for sexual freedom.

There is a section of publishers of pornography who consider themselves to be agents of the social revolution. Taking their cue from Reich and Marcuse, they claim that our society, being based upon sexual repression, will be undermined more effectively and fundamentally by the spreading of sexual freedom than by any other revolutionary activity. They claim that the propagation of sexual freedom is the most effective aspect of the revolutionary struggle, particularly at a time when the working class opposition is, to a great extent, bourgeoisified, i.e. absorbed into the establishment by the consumer-ethics.

Reich has declared that: "The suppression of the natural sex life of children and adolescents serves the function of structuring people to uphold and reproduce a mechanistic authoritarian (and oppressive) civilisation," and "the coming generation must under all circumstances and with all means be saved from being influenced by the biological rigidity of the old generation." [1]

This encourages some advocates of the alternative society to assert that there is no problem in pornography, as sex is one of the revolutionary weapons which would change society; promiscuity, provided the danger of V.D. and the need for contraception were pointed out, was a beneficial way of breaking up the family structure.

7. PORNOGRAPHY

I shall discuss later this idea of using sexuality as a weapon for revolution. A study of some 'underground' journals will reveal that they use sexual symbols not to propagate the freedom to love, but to ridicule, outrage and undermine not only existing mores but also the personal and affectionate aspects in human relationships. One gains the impression that what they defile is not so much the old order as sexuality itself. The aggressive and sadistic ambience which dominates these journals and which, far from liberating people from their repressions, stimulates sadistic and perverse impulses in those who are sympathetic, arouses disgust and resentment in others. Whether the defiant sadistic nature of their treatment of sex is deliberate in order to reinforce the reader's aggressive, rebellious disposition and to strengthen his defiance towards society, or whether it is motivated by a perverse syndrome amongst its editors, one can only leave to the readers to judge.

There is no doubt that various so-called radical parties are making deliberate use of this 'sexual liberation movement' and see it as a potent means by which to undermine the establishment.

Having got hold of some snippets of Reich, without in the least bothering to understand what he was about, despite his repeated and laboured warnings against his misinterpreters and exploiters, underground journals adopt the sexually repressed masses as the revolutionary vanguard in the struggle for liberation from capitalism and honour them as an oppressed class. Just like women and youth, so now the sexually repressed have to be made conscious of their oppression, have to be transformed into class-conscious revolutionary cadres. Opportunists and facile salesmen of a phoney revolution are engaged in exploiting the momentum of sexual change for their own ends.

It is not surprising that there have emerged a number of critics of the 'new freedom' who concentrate on the pornographic debasement of sexuality.

A critique of the sexual revolution should not, however, confine itself to an attack upon pornography. Pornography is not the chief culprit; it is merely the symptom of a disease that has deeply affected our civilisation. To say that pornography is evil and should be curtailed means condemning a symptom and ignoring the disease. Let us never forget that the disease was there long before the new pornographic freedom. What we are encountering in the Western world is the emergence into the open of sexual symptoms which, in the past, have been held in check by religious and authoritarian taboos. The patriarchal taboos have created the sickness of the sexual-biological system of man and then in turn repressed the symptoms. The new milieu of freedom merely permits symptoms to manifest themselves openly. It is true that many consider the free expression of sickness as a kind of health. There is a modicum of truth in this contention, but it is quite wrong on the whole, for sickness, if set as a standard, tends to perpetuate itself.

David Holbrook has recently written a number of books concerned with the new sexuality and its pornographic proliferation, but his attacks, while timely and no doubt sincere, miss the point. To quote one of his statements from his book *The Pseudo Revolution – A Critical Study of Extremist Liberation in Sex*: "The student of the true sexual revolution thus sees that the prime enemy is no longer the repressive anti-sexual social system but the repressive pornographic culture pattern." This is a far too simplistic view.

Of course some of the existential psychoanalysts like Viktor Frankl and Rollo May can be used to support a superficial view of the problem. One cannot, however, understand the present scene unless one is prepared to think radically about it, and the radical view of human behaviour includes the unconscious and infantile sexuality. As Freud said to Jung, when he still had some hope for him: "Promise me never to forget the unconscious and infantile sexuality, for without them the psychoanalytical theory is meaningless." Equally, if one is to make sense of the 'sexual revolution' in our time, its distortions and betrayals, its claims and counter-claims, we must realise that the major taboos which operate both in our culture as well as in our individual psyche are unconscious and have barely slackened their grip upon us. The changes in our conscious morality, and the weakening of our loyalty to the "old negator" and his authoritarian representatives, have not significantly affected our deep-lying fears, tensions and inhibitions. These are created in our childhood and continue to operate in our unconscious. The conscious mind, to a very great extent, merely acts as a rationalising and sublimating agency for our unconscious attitudes and even an ideology of freedom often harbours unconscious hatreds, fears, totem worship or compulsions, as we know all too well from history.

That the current worship of sexual freedom serves to satisfy a complex variety of infantile fixations and compulsions should not lead one to condemn freedom but to try to understand the difficulties we have in its realisation. We know that freedom movements and revolutionary aspirations have, with terrifying regularity, turned into repressive authoritarianism and have, all too often, released perverse and sadistic drives. Many people confronted with the truth of this human experience in history become cynical, start muttering about 'human nature' or become reactionary in the name of 'order and decency'.

The radical insights of psychoanalysis do not confirm a deterministic or misanthropic view of man, but attempt to explain the reasons for man's incapacity for freedom.

The failure of the sexual revolution, and its pornographic perverse manifestation, illustrate the emotional and sexual disease that is in us, and while we cannot but deplore these symptomatic manifestations, their observation may teach us something about the human sickness and how to overcome it.

The difficulty about protecting the genuine aspects of the sexual liberation from people who champion it chiefly as a means of living out their perverse secondary drives, lies in the problem of defining what we mean by healthy sexuality.

Let me give a short explanation of pornography from the point of view of the psycho-sexual development of the individual.

The libido deals with repression in two major ways. One is the dissociation of the ego from sexual drives, resulting in a sense of non-involvement, coldness, emptiness, as if the ego were to say – yes, there is such a thing as sexual desire but it has really nothing to do with me. I don't really feel it – it happens outside me. (I have mentioned this process of dissociation in Ch. 3.) This creates on the one hand an affect block and on the other a compulsion to engage in vicarious pleasure, an excitement in other people's sexual feelings which in turn, if repressed, creates mistrust, paranoid fantasies or free-floating anxiety. The other way of coping with repression consists in deflecting the libido backwards to earlier, infantile primacies, like sadism and masochism, narcissistic exhibitionism, anal and urethral sexuality. Under the pressure of the superego these regressive solutions are, in turn, repressed. As we know, they don't disappear but manifest themselves symbolically and symptomatically, i.e. in neuroses. As Freud repeatedly stressed: "Neuroses represent the symbolisation of repressed perversions."

Sado-masochistic urges and fantasies, if repressed, can create chronic depressions, melancholia, anorexia nervosa, and rigidities of the mind and body up to catatonia. Repressed exhibitionism can create acute shyness and social anxiety, palpitations and stage-fright. The love and desire for mother, if on the one hand strongly stimulated and at the same time denied, can turn into identification with her and to a wide range of homosexual and transvestite preoccupations which, if repressed, can cause inadequacy feelings, paranoid anxieties, masochistic compulsions and an overall sense of failure; urethral sensations can lead to compulsive crying, the denial of all pleasure sensations for fear that they may cause a crying attack, feelings of weakness, vertigo and falling compulsions, hysterical imagery of floating, loss of identity or of peripheral self-awareness. Fixations upon the anal libido can arouse a need to degrade, i.e. dirty everything and everybody by 'mudslinging and muckraking', or manifest itself in the hoarding instinct, the accumulation of money and wealth which, as we see, often goes with the devaluation of the world into things which are to be made use of and exploited. The constipated capitalist or autocrat are typical examples of this character-type.

These are just a few examples of the enormous variety of displacements and transformations of the libido which occur under the pressure of a libido-negating culture and, needless to say, these fixations and regressions appear in a multitude of symptoms and character traits.

A sexual liberation which has the liberation of pornography as its aim is a liberation of perversions, that is to say, of regres-

7. PORNOGRAPHY

sive fixations. When the "old negator" no longer commands moral authority in our conscious minds, then perversions need not be repressed and can come to the surface. They do so with a show of defiance and parade in a mad dance of victory over the old taboos and customs.

The cult of pornography satisfies to a degree the perverse or infantile needs of repressed people, but also keeps intact the taboos upon mature sexual relationships. It does not release the muscular rigidities of the inhibited person, nor his mental blocks. Pornography that goes under the name of liberation merely perpetuates the denial of love; it reinforces the sick and distorted sexuality of the man or woman who does not feel accepted.

We shall have occasion to see manifestations of infantile pregenital drives and their distortions in commercial and political pornography and in romantic literature. Let us however first see how pornography manifests itself in heterosexual relationships subjected to the taboos of patriarchy.

To define the word pornography: *porne* – whore, *graphein* – to write: description of the activities of whores. Whores are sexual commodities to be purchased by men whose sexual gratification with respectable women is either restricted or denied. Whores gratify an urge that is morally censored and needs to be repressed in the encounter with ordinary women. Ordinary women deny men sexual gratification in patriarchy and repress their own; whores do not negate sexuality upon suitable payment. Men lead a respectable life with ordinary women, i.e. they repress their sexual needs with them and lead an immoral life with prostitutes. 'Ordinary' women represent sexual aim-inhibition, whores represent sexual aim-fulfilment.

In the world of patriarchy where the Oedipus complex rules, the woman represents an object of desire and, at the same time, is the forbidden object. Only the whore is an object of sexual desire which is not forbidden, therefore she is immoral. Sexual gratification is sanctioned by God for the purpose of his glorification and the perpetuation of the establishment. The child is the gift-offering to God and subject to his commandments in return for the pleasures God has permitted in the act of procreation. The respectable woman symbolises the mother who negates her own sexual desires for the son (the young man); she protects him from temptation by her coyness and purity and so protects father's love for him. She thus keeps him within the moral laws, within his religion and the established system of authority. Should she allow men to love her freely then the whole edifice of patriarchy would break down and Father-God would either punish mankind in a paroxysm of rage or he would shrink into nothing.

In order to maintain a balance between natural urges and the requirements of the authoritarian social establishment, man has to split himself into two: the immoral, non-respectable animal and the moral, respectable citizen and God-worshipper who upholds the purity of his woman, but vents his animality upon the 'others'. Women also split themselves into the good woman, the wife and mother who is protected from her sexual drives by muscular rigidity and mental blocks, and the unconscious libertine who finds her representation in those women who enact what the respectable women does not.

Just as the establishment tolerates whores, so it tolerates pornography in order to relieve the tensions created by the sex-negating morality. It is partial release for sexual needs normally repressed, a channel of discharge which protects the establishment. As the 'respectable' person dissociates himself from the 'lower' sexual impulses, so the whore's sexuality is dissociated from her personality; she is the symbol of depersonalised sexuality. She is the 'other' woman who does not belong to patriarchal culture and therefore is immoral.

This was not always the case. In matriarchal society the priestess was a symbol of uninhibited sexual gratification and her worship was the affirmation and the celebration of the powers of woman. Sex then was holy, and sexual acts and sexual enjoyment the magic representation of man's love for the female principle, sexual gratification the fertilising fulfilment of the needs of mother-earth. In patriarchy and particularly Christianity the priestess became the witch, the whore, just as the God of Fertility became the devil. What was sacred in matriarchal paganism became profane in patriarchy, what was holy became sinful. The fertility rites and sexual symbolisations became, in patriarchy, pornography. But while the conscious moral person-

7. PORNOGRAPHY

ality, being dominated by the patriarchal superego, must repress the matriarchal cult of sexual desire and fulfilment, it cannot entirely stop it but will dissociate itself in its moral and conscious thinking from it, and so the pursuit of pleasure becomes lust, a sinful, immoral and degraded activity.

1. Wilhelm Reich: *The Biological Miscalculation in the Human Struggle for Freedom* (International Journal of Sex-Economy, Vol. 2, 1943).

8. *Romanticism*

There is, however, another approach – one that does not depersonalise woman but on the contrary emphasises and glorifies her personality. This is romantic love, which has played and continues to play an important role in European Christian civilisation. It has often been said that the spiritualisation of woman in romantic love is a form of sexual sublimation. This is partly true, but it is far more than that. If we consider that passion is an important aspect of romantic love and that passion often assumes a morbid and perverse form, then we must look for a deeper significance in romanticism. The romantic movement in Europe represented a temporary breakthrough of matriarchy, the worship of woman as a goddess, when men feel the restraints of their male God to be intolerable. There have been certain periods in history when men rebelled against him and invoked the ancient goddess of liberty, love and pleasure and worshipped her. The repressed libido, as we know, does not disappear either in individuals or in cultures, but leads an underground existence. It is ready to break through the surface of repressions at times of psychological and cultural crises.

The worship of the female principle, symbolised by matriarchy, has never been eliminated or completely conquered by patriarchy, but merely repressed, continuing to exist as an unconscious, dormant culture, side by side with the dominant culture of patriarchy. The interrelationship between the deities of patriarchy and of matriarchy is complex, and their battle for dominance plays an important part in the drama of European religion, art and literature.

We might say that the whole edifice of patriarchal culture is an attempt to resolve the Oedipus conflict; it represents a turning towards the Father-God in order to seek his love and forgiveness for the original sin of incestuous desire for the mother, a restitution of his power and his glory after his (unconscious) murder by the son. Submission to his will, the worship of order and purity and the repression of sexual fantasies and yearnings which disrupt the patriarchal order, have become man's highest duty; but at the same time, the longing for the love of woman, for her world of affection and her softness rebels against the demands of purity and order.

The daemonic sensibility articulated by Goethe and worshipped by Byron is nothing less than the worship of the female principle, held in check by the worship of God, the male. "Das ewig Weibliche zieht uns hinan," declared Goethe at the end of his heroic masterpiece *Faust*. At the end of all the conflicts of Western man there is this fundamental truth: "The eternal feminine beckons to us and draws us towards it." But the women of patriarchy have themselves repressed the female principle of love, affection and sexual pleasure. In order to be accepted by patriarchal culture, they have had to surround themselves with an armour of respectability which hides their libido. They had to deny their own Goddess and submit to an alien God. Patriarchal woman is a victim who represents the defeat of her goddess by Jehovah. But not quite. She still has the secret affection of Jehovah who consorts with her in the holy of holies of the Temple (the bedroom) which no man (son) may enter or even see, and she still commands the hidden longing of the sons. At certain periods in history the libido of matriarchy breaks through the patriarchal restrictions and evokes adoration of the female and a passion for her, a passion dictated by the desire to break down the barriers of her respectability and liberate her from her own restraints.

We find three main variants in all romantic movements, namely: adoration, sadism and masochism. The breakthrough of matriarchal orientations created at various periods an upsurge of an alternative sensibility, particularly in literature, although it has found its way into the other arts as well, and has had a complex impact upon ideology and politics.

In the twelfth century and in the nineteenth century and again now, romanticism has emerged as a powerful force in the human imagination. The literature of chivalry of the troubadours, of *Tristan and Isolde*, Dante and Petrarch, is a source of delight and inspiration that has called forth a profusion of learned books and articles. The nineteenth century romantic themes of Salomé, the Medusa, La Belle Dame sans Merci, Romantic poets like Keats, Byron, Baudelaire, Flaubert, Mallarmé, Swinburne, the curious figure of the Marquis de Sade, Wilde and many others, have become part of the contradictory and baffling heritage of the European culture. The contemporary symbols and exponents of the Romantic movement, however, are still too near to be properly understood and discerned.

In the twelfth century the outpourings of the romantic sensibility were accompanied by Mary-worship in Christianity, which transformed the symbols and rituals of the Church in many countries of Europe. Madonna worship was certainly a manifestation of matriarchal orientations and became a focal point of religious feelings.

The romantic adoration and spiritualisation of woman is based upon a deep compassion for the loved woman who is a victim of God, a victim of the male, the Mater Dolorosa, and her suffering and her purity are idealised in a declaration of loyalty, a kind of covenant with her. The sweet sadness, the melancholy feeling of loyalty to the woman who is the victim of a God strange to her, the sadness for her imprisonment by convention is deeply felt by her worshippers and expressed in poems with a lyricism and beauty unequalled in the history of Europe and still now considered to be the summit of poetic accomplishment. But the woman to whom the poet declares his undying love, his allegiance for life, is sexually unattainable to him. To the romantic, marriage denies real love. It is perforce the negation of passion, it is to him unholy, whereas the covenant of romantic love is the true passion. It creates suffering and melancholy as well as rage, it spurs the romantic lover to heroic deeds, to his inevitable self-destruction.

"My Lords, if you would hear a high tale of love and death," thus begins the epic story of *Tristan and Iseult*. As Denis de Rougemont writes: "Love and death, a fatal love – in these phrases is summed up, if not the whole of poetry, at least what-

8. ROMANTICISM

ever is popular, whatever is universally moving in European literature, alike as regards the oldest legends and the sweetest songs. Happy love has no history. Romance only comes into existence where love is fatal, frowned upon and doomed by life itself. What stirs lyrical poets to their finest flights is neither the delight of the senses nor the fruitful contentment of the settled couple; not the satisfaction of love but its passion. And passion means suffering. There we have the fundamental fact." [1]

The common view that courtly love romance is but the idealisation of sexual desire, is justified to some extent by the writings of Geoffrey Rudel, Prince of Bly, a famous troubadour who states quite clearly that his lady is a creation of his mind and that "she vanishes at dawn and what the body denies me the spirit grants." In Geoffrey Rudel's poetry we find many realistic descriptions of a certain lady who does not appear merely as a symbol, and there are straightforward passages of sexual desire – some brutally frank even by our standards. But it will be seen that the spiritual elaboration of her beauty and desirability fires the imagination and stimulates desire and leads to a sexualisation of the spirit.

The love that is devoted to the 'Lady', who is very often married, has its sadistic as well as masochistic components. Already Rambaut of Orange, another twelfth-century troubadour, declares in a poem that if you want to win women, you should be brutal to them, "punch them on the nose, force them, because that is what they like." In the poetry of the German Minnesinger von Lichtenberg, we see the idolisation of women brought to such a pitch of exaggeration that many of his readers gained the impression that he wished to satirise and ridicule the romantic movement.

While the adoration of woman is the main subject of the poetry of the troubadours, very soon there emerges the cult of an erotic sensibility in which sexual passion is the central preoccupation. The male, fired by images of the beautiful lady, endeavours to break through the sexual barriers that surround her; he has to overcome and destroy her resistances, and there appears in the literature of romantic love the image of the satanic destroyer of women's purity. He has to be sadistic to gain sexual access to the pure and negating woman. She then becomes the victim, the delicate fragile creature injured by the wild and ruthless passions of the male – the sadist, the satanist, the outlaw, the robber – who conquers woman's defences and destroys her will.

In the nineteenth century this figure plays a large role in Romantic literature. But already in the fourteenth century in the poetry of Dante and even Petrarch, the greatest lover of all time, this theme emerges. Petrarch expresses in his poetry all three stages of romantic love: spiritual adoration, intimations of Satanism and suffering unto death. Here is Petrarch's sonnet on the first anniversary of his love for Laura:

> And still I bless the day, the hour, the place,
> When first so high mine eyes I dared to rear;
> And say, 'Fond heart, thy gratitude to declare,
> That then thou had'st the privilege to gaze.'
> 'Twas she inspired the tender thought of love
> Which points to heaven, and teaches to despise
> The earthly vanities that others prize:
> She gave the soul's light grace, which to the skies
> Bids thee straight onward in the right path move;
> Whence bouy'd by hope e'en now I soar to worlds above.

Joy and the suffering of passion is exquisitely expressed by him in many poems:

> O vivid lustre! of power absolute
> O'er all my being – source of that delight
> By which consumed I sink, a willing prey.
>
> Oh breathing death! yet ill I joy to feel!
> Unsanction'd thus to rule, oh! whence thy art?

and again:

> And thus my martyrdom no limit knows,
> A thousand deaths and lives each day I feel.

Satan, that God-fallen victim of Jehovah's conquest, the natural lover, untainted by patriarchal restrictions, is described with admiration by Milton. For him "the evil one" assumes an aspect of fallen beauty, of great splendour shadowed by sadness and death. He is "majestic" though in ruins. Blake's declaration that Milton himself was of the devil's party without knowing it, and the question whether Satan's cry of revolt is the cry of the poet himself has been debated for centuries. In any case it cannot be denied that the character of Satan in *Paradise Lost* expresses something in which Milton believed very strongly: heroic energy.

Schiller observes on the subject of *Paradise Lost*: "Automatically the reader would take the side of the loser; an artifice by which Milton, the panegyrist of Hell transforms for a moment even the mildest of readers into a fallen angel." Shelley in his *Defence of Poetry* goes further: "Milton's poem contains within itself a philosophical refutation of that system of which, by a strange and natural antithesis, it has been a chief popular support. Nothing can exceed the energy and magnificence of the character of Satan as expressed in *Paradise Lost*. It is a mistake to suppose that he could ever have been intended for the popular personification of evil ... Milton's devil as a moral being is far superior to his God as one who perseveres in some purpose, which he has conceived to be excellent, in spite of adversity and torture, is one who in the cold security of undoubted triumph inflicts the most horrible revenge upon his enemy with the alleged design of exasperating him to deserve new torments." Milton's undoubted identification with Satan as the hero represents a romantic rebellion against the image of man, subdued and humble towards a God whose exercise of power is far from being admirable.

Milton's Satan, observes Mario Praz, is immediately recognisable in the shrewd portrait of Byron outlined by the Earl of Lovelace in *Astarte*, the first book to throw light on the mystery of the life of his grandfather the poet: "He had a fancy for some Oriental legends of pre-existence, and in his conversation and poetry took up the part of a fallen or exiled being, expelled from heaven, or sentenced to a new avatar on earth for some crime, existing under a curse, pre-doomed to a fate really fixed by himself in his own mind, but which he seemed determined to fulfil.

At times this dramatic imagination resembled a delusion: he would play at being mad and gradually get more and more serious, as if he believed himself to be destined to wreck his own life and that of everyone near him."[2] In the stanzas of *Lara*, Byron reproduces the sombre portrait of his idealised self:

> There was in him a vital scorn of all:
> As if the worst had fall'n which could befall,
> He stood a stranger in this breathing world,
> An erring spirit from another hurl'd;
> A thing of dark imaginings, that shaped
> By choice the perils he by chance escaped;
> But 'scaped in vain, for in the memory yet
> His mind would half exult and half regret:
> With more capacity for love than earth
> Bestows on most of mortal mould and birth,
> His early dreams of good outstripp'd the truth,
> And troubled manhood follow'd baffled youth;
> With thought of years in phantom chase misspent,
> And wasted powers for better purpose lent;
> And fiery passions that had pour'd their wrath
> In hurried desolation o'er his path,
> And left the better feelings all at strife
> In wild reflection o'er his stormy life;
> But haughty still, and loth himself to blame,
> He call'd on Nature's self to share the shame,
> And charged all faults upon the fleshly form
> She gave to clog the soul, and feast the worm ...

To transcend the limitations imposed by culture, to be free from restraints that encumber the common souls, is a quest that drove Faust, Don Juan and Raskolnikov to their salvation and their doom. They have to destroy in order to feel alive and free. They have to break down the barriers which encumber the experience of love: "My embrace was fatal – I loved her, and destroyed her."[3] Even in the simplest of his works Byron obstructs the course of love by means of a prohibition. Straightforward sensations were not enough for him. He was never so satisfied as when he saw shadows of death blighting the marriage bed.[4]

8. ROMANTICISM

It is worth noting that for individuals aware of the inhibitions and restrictions imposed upon them by the taboos of patriarchy, enormous passions are necessary in order to experience the sensations of living. Byron had to key up his life to a high state of tension for it to yield him anything. But when it came to his post-mortem it was found that both brain and heart showed signs of very advanced age: the sutures of the brain were entirely obliterated and the heart bore signs of incipient ossification. Yet Byron was only 36. Is not this extraordinary condition of his brain and his heart due to a shrinking parapathy brought about by incestuous guilt and anxiety, and did he not have to conquer both his parapathy as well as his inhibitions by breaking through the boundaries of normalcy? That is to say, of acquiescence in patriarchy? The woman he wanted had to be conquered and defeated, in order to yield herself to him, and he had to conquer his own inhibitions and experience a paroxysm of passion that signified to him the sensation of being alive.

Through one of his characters the Marquis de Sade declares: "I have destroyed everything in my heart that stood in the way of my pleasure." He attempted to break down the resistances offered to man by the civilised woman and, what is more, had to destroy the image of her resistance, and the whole of the morality that promoted it. He did not succeed in establishing a genital loving relationship with another person but could experience passion only with the degraded wreck of what was a person. And by doing so he degraded himself as he well knew. But even his self-degradation expressed the denial of the accepted morality and, in this, he considered himself victorious.

As the other side of sadism is masochism, so the cult of Satanism has its counterpart in the worship of the fatal woman, 'La Belle Dame sans Merci'. Here the delicate and vulnerable beauty turns into the fierce avenger, not only against the sadism of individual males but against the whole male-dominated negation of her freedom and identity. She appears in two aspects. On the one hand she represents the mother who tempts the boy into transgression of the sexual taboo, and then punishes him for it – she is the teaser, the double-bind figure, who desires love and promises to give it and then betrays him to the father: Eve, the temptress, who brings down upon men God's wrath and causes their expulsion from the paradise of innocence. Then there is the pre-patriarchal woman, the mother-figure who does not submit to her husband or God, does not accept his restrictions and arouses and frightens the young man with her sexuality, asserts her sexual powers over men, defeats their culture and their pride: Lilith, the matriarchal Goddess, who mocks God and in Hebrew literature is depicted as the beautiful harlot who seduces men and tramples on them.

Let us remember that the man who himself is the victim of the inhibitions and rigidities imposed by patriarchal negations often wants a sadistic woman to penetrate his armour and release his blocked passions. Her claws and her teeth are symbols of salvation and his suffering an experience of sexual gratification:

> For all Christ's work this Venus is not quelled,
> But reddens at the mouth with blood of men,
> Sucking between small teeth the sap o' the veins,
> Dabbling with death her little tender lips –
> A bitter beauty, poisonous-pearled mouth ...
> ... Ah, fair love,
> Fair fearful Venus made of deadly foam,
> I shall escape you somehow with my death.[5]

Let me again quote from Swinburne who plays a significant role in nineteenth-century Romanticism. He expresses in powerful imagery the morbid passions of the movement:

> ... the strange woman, she the flower, the sword,
> Red from spilt blood, a mortal flower to men,
> Adorable, detestable.

The romantic masochist uses the sadistic woman to free him from the prison of his superego, from the affect block it has imposed upon him, and wants her to penetrate his defences, tear them to shreds, mock them, trample them under foot and make him suffer, for only in this pain of suffering can he find his orgastic release. While the romantic masochist wants the woman's personality and her will to overpower his own resistances and his morality, the romantic sadist wants to overpower the woman's moral resistances and, in this way, to liberate her sexuality.

In both these cases we can witness an effort of the libido to break through the affect block that prevents it from finding discharge or outlet, just as the infant, when confronted by the cold or indifferent breast, develops sadistic urges and will attack it with its teeth and nails, not in order to destroy the breast, i.e. the mother, but to destroy and remove the resistant layers of her personality and to release the libido in her and gain access to it. When the child experiences the warmth of the mother's body, the love of her person and her admiration which communicates through her body and her movements, and shows in her eyes, then the child feels its own libido and is aware of its own personality and identity. It feels loving and loved, accepted and accepting; it can communicate its love through warmth and affection. Should these rhythms of affection of body and mind be broken – and they are broken in our culture with its crazy restraint upon the experience of the pleasure felt in the contact with the child, or person one loves – then the feel of our bodies, our movements and the light in our eyes are dimmed and are cold and mechanical. The child will feel resentment and aggression and often the only pleasure it can experience is the pleasure of nastiness and aggression; sadism will emerge as the only channel by which the libido can express itself.

Thus aggression and sadism are the constant companions of man in our culture. The superego frightens our parents, our brothers and sisters and prevents them from experiencing the natural pleasure of human contact. Having made us love-starved sadists, our gods direct their black looks upon us and belabour us about our sinful nature. They make us submit to their higher will in order to sacrifice our evil selves. Their will is to be done by obeying orders from the authorities that operate in their name. A life of order and discipline is required from us to restrain our natural and our secondary drives. Freedom is a word that figures in all the agendas, but it is merely a freedom to believe and to think what we are told to feel and think. *Their* rules and their expectations, the higher purposes which are held up to us are inscribed in our faith, and ingrained in our culture. We try to obey, and submit, but almost always fail to do so properly, poor sinners that we are. Our culture and our faith are both a medium through which they (the voices from on high – from heaven, the pulpit, or the ruler's balcony) speak to us, and exhort us, but they also give us that feeling of happiness that comes from being accepted by them. But when men begin to lose faith in the ancient and hereditary gods, when the voice from on high fails to command our loyalty then, as Benedetto Croce has said:

> "The impressionable, sentimental and fickle minds, having lost sight of the true God made to themselves idols ... they identified the infinite with this or that finite, the ideal with this or that perceptible; and there resulted from this those exaggerations, usurpations, and in fact subversions of values which are more properly called perversions: lust and voluptuousness put in place of ideals, cruelty and horror flavoured with sensual pleasure, a taste for incest, sadism, Satanism and other amusements of that kind – altogether monstrous and stupid. It was thus that not a few of the Romantics, having failed either to subdue or to pacify by their own strength of mind the upheaval which they had aroused in their own breasts, or to rise above it by forgetting it and returning to their humble everyday lives, went to perdition."

Thus, Benedetto Croce on the romantic sensibility of the nineteenth century when erotic longing began to invade the consciousness of sensitive minds, who would no longer capitulate to the "old negator" and his duty-bound "female eunuchs", the distant and coy Madonnas that went by the name of woman:

> Ah beautiful passionate body
> That never has ached with a heart!
> On thy mouth though the kisses are bloody,
> Though they sting till it shudder and smart,
> More kind than the love we adore is,
> They hurt not the heart or the brain,

8. ROMANTICISM

O bitter and tender Dolores,
  Our Lady of Pain. [6]

The God of civilisation and the civilised woman could no longer contain the rage and sexual longing that was in man; they burst forth in the nineteenth century breaking the moulds of civilised values and flooded the European sensibility with images so strange and unfamiliar, so exotic and wild and yet always dormant in the private fantasies of Western man. They articulated what men of inferior sensibility could only harbour in their breasts and their loins with shame and horror – the consciousness of the daemonic in the art and the literature of the Western world, in its surrealism, in its chaotic negation of order, in its perversions, which demanded the revaluation of all values:

There are sins it may be to discover,
There are deeds it may be to delight.
What new work wilt thou find for thy lover,
What new passions for daytime or night?
What spells that they know not a word of
Whose lives are as leaves overblown?
What tortures undreamt of, unheard of,
  Unwritten, unknown? [7]

Goethe, Schiller, Byron, Keats, Swinburne, Nietzsche, Baudelaire, Gautier, Huysmans, Wilde, Gide, and many others evolved the new imagery which in its varied manifestations goes by the name of Romantic. The force that produced the romantic agony was the libido held back by centuries of denial imposed by Christian authoritarianism, by the iron will of the ancient God, the psychic and bodily armour which he forged around the people we wish to love – the decent women, the good mothers and fathers, our friends and associates who walk in a shadow and whose eyes and gestures reveal the great denial: all those who make us strangers to the joy and love that we crave for.

The themes of decadence are continuing in our time. The nineteenth-century romanticism gave birth to revolutionary movements which have endeavoured to provide an answer to the discontents of European civilisation. The romantic rebellion turned into a political revolution for, however unpolitical the romantic movement seemed to the politically minded, it expressed and, at the same time, furthered, the downfall of the old order. The romantics were already the gravediggers of the bourgeoisie and its philistine values long before the 'practical' people realised the spiritual emptiness of the social order. Today we face the revolutions which have created new Gods that once more stifle the human sensibility and we face a world which, though revolutionary in its technological and scientific aspects, has become dehumanised. The libido longs for another breakthrough against values which in their worship of mechanical efficiency and bureaucratic order have reinstated the "old negator" of patriarchy in a new guise. We have a world which, on the one hand, is governed by a technological totalitarianism and, on the other hand, presents a new romanticism of anti-order, of chaotic disintegration and regression to infantilism.

The new romanticism manifests a retreat from articulation, its symbols are of an altogether lower mental order. The evocative line of poetry is being replaced by the blatant cliché of the advertisers' mentality and by the imagery of the strip cartoon. The fantasies expressed in literature, painting and sculpture are being replaced by erotic photography and monosyllabic language. The reductionism that operates in the sciences of man and in modern mass literature and journalism has taken over, and the erotic sensibility appears as mass-produced pornography.

I have earlier pointed out the difference between politically unpretentious commercial pornography and that which claims ideological and political significance. It is interesting to note that the more ideologically-minded it claims to be, the more technically and literally crude it becomes, and the more pronounced the predominance of sado-masochism. The disruptive intentions of the political pornographer are directed against the order and the laws of the patriarchal establishment, and the traditional forms of sexuality. He denies affection and love and emphasises sadism as a form of breaking through the established order and its norms of civilised behaviour; he is masochistic insofar as he consciously or preconsciously worships the avenging female goddess. The overwhelming Lilith is much featured; the woman who hates men and exercises her power over them also hates the traditional establishment of patriarchal order and is therefore worshipped. Flagellation and sexual domination by the female is profusely depicted in pictures, photomontage and cartoons. While the commercial pornography represents an alienated shop window type of sexual stimulation, the political pornography shows aspects of morbidity and perversion which recalls the Romanticists of the last century, albeit in a regressive, intellectually decadent manner. Where romantic morbidity employed the highest forms of intellectual articulation, its contemporary counterpart expresses itself in the form of puerile graffiti, customary on lavatory walls, but new in journals and books.

1. Denis de Rougemont: *Passion and Society* (London: Faber, 1990).
2. Mario Praz: *The Romantic Agony* (Fontana, 1971).
3. Lord Byron: *Manfred*, Act II.
4. Mario Praz: *The Romantic Agony* (Fontana, 1971).
5. Algernon Charles Swinburne: *Chastelard*, a Tragedy (1865), Act V, Scene 2.
6. Algernon Charles Swinburne: 'Dolores'.
7. *Ibid.*

9. The Journalism of Pornography

Let us now briefly review the journalism of commercial pornography. The most popular of the sex magazines, if popularity be judged by circulation are, without doubt, *Playboy* and *Penthouse*. These journals, while having a large coverage of sexual titillation, also devote space to other topics of interest and this applies particularly to *Playboy*. It contains a section on books, not all restricted to pornography, and has included reviews of such books as: *Luce and His Empire*; *Kissinger: The Uses of Power*; *The FBI and the Berrigans*, and also books like *The Joy of Sex*, which offers sound counsel on hang-ups as well as some homely household hints, as for instance 'On sex in the shower' – "Don't pull down the fixture ... it isn't weight-bearing," or 'On semen' – "You can get it out of clothing or furnishings either with a stiff brush, when the stain has dried, or with a diluted solution of sodium bicarbonate." The book's emphasis is of course on "getting and giving the greatest pleasure through a smorgisbord of sophisticated lovemaking techniques" (approached with an attitude of try it if you like it).

There is a major feature entitled '*Playboy* Forum' – an interchange of ideas between reader and editor on subjects raised by the *Playboy* philosophy. There are readers' letters which concern themselves with a large range of topics on sex, such as birth control, doctors' attitudes to it, nymphomaniacs, peculiar sex habits, as well as with other American topics, often of a political nature. The tone of the letters and the answers to them represent a mildly liberal and anti-establishment attitude. While *Playboy* disagrees with certain illiberal aspects of the law and shows sympathy with readers who are baffled or disturbed by it, it is careful to take a stance of enlightened prudence.

9. THE JOURNALISM OF PORNOGRAPHY

Playboy magazine is associated with '*Playboy* Clubs', an industry devoted to providing a sexually wholesome and pleasant atmosphere. There are, as far as I know, six of these establishments in the United States, and a number spread all over the world. The *Playboy* Club provides an atmosphere of comfort and relaxation with all the mod cons American civilisation can provide. The Bunny Girls capture the spirit of the 'playboy' perfectly. They are cosy intimations of the boy's playthings – his bunny rabbits and teddy bears – wistfully remembered by the middle-aged tycoon, cherished and affectionately gazed upon with a mixture of nostalgia and hints of sexual pleasure without any commitment.

One can even see in the *Playboy* culture a spirit equivalent to nineteenth century middle-class liberalism that opposed authoritarianism while careful not to undermine the establishment that laid the golden eggs and kept them comfortable in their clubs. But while the liberals of the nineteenth century needed the principles of individual liberty, freedom of the press and *laissez-faire* and an ideology of progress to break the vested interests of feudal authority and religious superstition, the new exponents of liberalism carry the gentle goddess of pleasure on their semi-ideological banner to create a focus for their identity. The worship of the good life and its bunny goddess of playful amusement is, however, careful to avoid any radical confrontation with prevailing values. The business man, the manager and technocrat, the Corporation men whose actual pursuits are ruthless and unbending in the chase after financial success, like to see themselves as innocent playboys, deserving relaxation and easy conversation as the reward for their good work, and *Playboy* Club and the gentle and untouchable bunnies are there to provide it.

A somewhat more demanding and outgoing approach to the pleasures of living is provided by the magazine *Penthouse* which has, in the last few years, overtaken *Playboy* in popularity. It projects a younger image: the youngish meritocrat who is out to get what he wants – material wealth, prestige and women, without the middle-aged restraints of bunny rabbit fantasies and bourgeois respectability. His prestige comes from go-getting: "You are reading this magazine because you are a demanding, perceptive man. You are not satisfied with getting it now and then. You expect your copy of *Penthouse* every month without fail." Nobody is misled by the pun; *Penthouse* readers really mean it. The journal differs from *Playboy* in its uninhibited display of nude photographs. Besides the centre double-page photograph of the '*Penthouse* pet of the month', it shows a great number of nude photographs, all in colour, and most of them full-page. The journal is of a technical excellence, quite up to the standard of *Playboy* and the quality of its photographs is probably the best among the journals of sexual titillation.

If we look at the January 1973 issue, for instance, we find three articles: one on plastic surgery, another of an interview with Robert Conquest, the sociologist. Robert Conquest gives details of "enormities – sexual and otherwise" committed in the name of political ideology. The emphasis on sex crimes against female political prisoners is unusual in an interview of this kind, but certainly in keeping with the interests of readers of *Penthouse,* even while the disclosures by Robert Conquest must be considered to be of general interest. The article on cosmetic surgery by Ivor and Sally Davis describes the boom in this field which is "outstripping psychiatrists from the front rank of modish medicine." The third article is frankly pornographic describing the amorous entanglements of jazz star Charlie Mingus and is entitled 'The Private Life of a Super Spade'. As the editorial (entitled Housecall) explains: "Jazz music was of course from its earliest days associated with bordellos and what used to be called loose living, and the great Louis Armstrong's first wife was a dance-hall whore. The very word 'jazz' means fornication in negro slang." A fictitious story entitled: 'The Fearful Fate of Don Pedro II', the extraordinary story of a young Spaniard who grew a second penis and finds that this misfortune brings him great fame and wealth due to the fascination aroused by it among the ladies in Spain and many other parts of the world.

The editors of *Penthouse* consider it a great journalistic scoop to have obtained the services of Xaviera Hollander, whose notorious memoirs entitled *The Happy Hooker* has sold more than three million copies in the United States. "Miss Hollander has agreed to contribute regular and exclusive sex advice to *Pent-

9. THE JOURNALISM OF PORNOGRAPHY

house readers ... it is safe to say that there has never been anything like it in journalism before, an unabashed bedroom Baedeker by a guide of unchallengeable familiarity with the surroundings."

In the '*Penthouse* Forum' editors and readers discuss topics arising out of *Penthouse*, its contents, its aspirations, and its areas of interest. This feature airs a great variety of fantasies and sexual peculiarities, and provides readers and contributors with a sense of belonging to a circle of similar-minded people under the benevolent protection and encouragement of the institute. *Penthouse* also has a special off-shoot in a manual called *Forum* which is chiefly devoted to these correspondence exchanges. As in *Playboy*, there is much talk about their 'philosophy', which is partly an American euphemism for a way of life as symbolised by the business company that can claim the loyalty and support of its employees and customers. That a company is there to make profit is taken for granted, indeed it is part of its philosophy but, above and beyond that, it must be able to claim that its commodities contribute to the happiness of mankind. Americans are not like Europeans content with making something to sell – they have to persuade themselves that they, at the same time, further the general good. What *Playboy* and *Penthouse* produce is a make-believe world with some of its beauties parading in the pictorial sideshow. Join the circle of regulars and you receive the badge of membership. You become a man who knows what life is all about.

Penthouse features on a large scale advertisements for sex-promoting commodities. It runs a *Penthouse* Book Society and advertises the literature in all its issues. There are books on erotic art, one entitled *The Sensuous Woman,* another on *Oragenitalism* – "the first and last word on oral sex", a *Pictorial Manual of Sexual Intercourse*, and others. There are advertisements for 'Judy – the instant girlfriend: her skin is a warm fleshlike vinyl that makes humans almost robotic: her social tastes are universal, and, her most breathless wish: BUY ME.' (£7, p & p free). There are the usual dildos, vaginal stimulants (one with 'four interchangeable heads for a whirlpool of pleasure'), duo balls from ancient Japan, creams for all sorts of sexual purposes, a condom in black (for funerals or when in mourning?) and penis energising rings, and other commodities.

Let us now turn to the less pretentious journals of commercial pornography, which don't fall behind in the proselytising of the good life of sexual stimulation.

'You never had it so good' exclaims the full-page advert on the back cover of *Knave Special* inviting readers to 'send for our fascinating catalogue of sexual aids and find out.' A company advertising the 'numerous helpful and satisfying aids intended to give greater fulfilment to the sexual act,' is an offshoot of *Knave* magazine which is published in London. This magazine announces its 1973 editions in the following manner:

> "In 1973 *Knave* will be bigger – 84 pages containing 300% more colour on which to present a new concept in erotic photography. A moving paper fantasy featuring girls more beautiful than your dreams in voluptuous extravaganza. All this set between superb features, good humour, biting satire and unashamed erotica. An unequalled sensual experience has arrived."

We, on our side, have in our tour of the red-light district of journalism arrived at the area entirely devoted to pornography and the promotion of sensual experience without attempts to cater for other aspects of life. The conversation here is entirely devoted to sex; the ambience is designed merely for sexual stimulation through pictures, readers' letters and articles. To heighten excitement with occasional forages into proselytising self-justification is the sole aim.

Knave contains about thirty nude photographs, mostly in colour, articles and short stories all about various aspects of sex. There is a leading feature entitled 'Contact' which, in the manner of '*Penthouse* Forum' consists of a collection of readers' letters. Advertisements are entirely devoted to sex commodities and sex literature. An article entitled 'Sex in America' describes how the sexual revolution has transformed America from a relatively puritan country into one that has "sex on the brain. There is hardly a town in the whole country that has not been affected by

9. THE JOURNALISM OF PORNOGRAPHY

the sexual revolution." After describing the prevalence of sex and its commercial trappings in the big cities, and the ease with which it is available in all forms and varieties, it concludes surprisingly that "there are still some one hundred and ninety million Americans treating sex as if Rebecca and Sunny Brook Farm still lived." This obviously leads to the hopeful conclusion that there is still a vast untapped market ready for exploitation.

The readers' letters in the feature entitled 'Contact' display much more openly than in the previous journals reviewed sexual fantasies which are often quite openly perverse. One is a letter by a 50-year-old woman who introduced a young boy into the pleasures of transvestism and describes her own sexual excitement which he arouses in her when wearing women's clothes: "For two years we have had the most wonderful sexual times together. I get wet between my legs just looking at him in girl's things and although he has plenty of undies of his own, he still loves to try on my things, particularly my knickers." Other letters describe the sexual excitement to be had from seeing a girl swimming in the water in her undies: "We found the sight of her getting out of the water with bra and pants clinging wetly to her and transparent was a most erotic sight." The writer of this letter advises readers to get their girl friends to go swimming with an ordinary bra and pants set, eulogising again the excitement when she gets out of the water. One letter describes a complicated vibrator which the male writer has made for himself and the enormously increased excitement it produced. He also made one for his lady friend so that they can arrange a climax at the same time.

Other letters are of the straightforward graffiti kind, telling in some detail the excitement of some sexual encounters. These run the gamut of fantasies and perversions which in the past were only communicated, if at all, among close friends or in small groups of males where there is often one fellow who likes to regale the company with outrageous stories of sexual adventures. In these journals we find such tales of fantasy and imagination or recollections of exciting situations, presented to the public as a whole, providing stimulation for the reader and satisfaction to the letter-writer, who knows that thousands will share his excitement. These readers' forums have become an important feature of all the pornographic journals, and provide the central reading matter in the sexual handbooks like *Forum, Intra, Janus* and others, which I shall mention later.

We can ask whether the writers of these little testaments to their sexual yearnings represent a vanguard of liberation that is breaking through the restraint of patriarchal repressions and fraudulent morality. Do they, in Wilhelm Reich's phrase, affirm the free, healthy life manifestations of men and women? Or do they represent merely the attempt of exhibitionists to excite thousands of voyeurists? The fashion of public self-exposure in these journals gives an opportunity for the release of pent-up fantasies, and it may be considered beneficial for readers to learn that they are not isolated in their fantasies, that they can share them with others.

We must, furthermore, acknowledge that all of us, male and female, harbour a whole host of genital and pre-genital, normal and perverse, heterosexual and homosexual fantasies but, according to our personality development, our fixations and ego structures, certain of them are predominant while others remain latent. If a person's dominant fantasies evoke particularly strong guilt feelings he will feel 'different' or isolated. Feeling guilty or bad, he is inhibited in his personal relationships and will try to find alternative outlets for his desires, and exhibitionism is one such outlet. Exhibitionists are isolated persons whose superego restrictions prevent them from communicating their sexual urges overtly towards another person of their own, or the other sex. They are afraid of the superego and hate it at the same time, and they need to defy it by an exhibitionistic act. Their main gratification comes from outraging the taboos or customs of their society and in tainting others with their forbidden sexuality. They want others to look and become excited through looking, and in this way also to defy the taboo. The act of looking, or listening, to forbidden sexual occurrences is a sort of infection of previously innocent or self-righteous people with forbidden sexuality. These exhibitionists create a community of defiance, be it two people – the exhibitor and voyeur – or large numbers of exhibitionists and voyeurs who, in their mutual act, defeat

9. THE JOURNALISM OF PORNOGRAPHY

the superego taboos. They hate the superego and its defeat provides considerable sexual excitement.

It is significant that the more defiant these people are and the more hostility they feel towards respectability, the more perverse their sexual tales become. Stories of love and happiness degenerate under the pressure of the forbidding authoritarian superego into tales of forbidden sexuality: they boast not of their love but of their perverse and outrageous experiences and invoke the approval and support of their fellows. By tainting their fellows with erotic tales and by evoking a response in them they transform them into fellow rebels against the traditional norm. These exhibitionists are, in a small or large way, gang leaders against the repressive superego. They incite their brothers to rebel against the sex-negating authority and to assert their sexual rights, their pleasure with the female whose sex was hidden from them and denied them. They lead an invasion of the bedroom to see her possessed by father, to chase him out and degrade him so that all the brothers can have pleasure with her. The defeat of father – his symbolic murder by the brothers – is not, as Freud assumed, a prehistoric event but is acted out every day in the fantasies of the repressed males of patriarchy. When we look at the modern scene we find that these little forums represent centres of sexual defiance. Their proselytising attitude is in keeping with the urge to create a community of brothers out to defeat the repressive establishment. But the journalistic establishment exploits the sexual rebellion. It employs journalists and experts and invites graffiti writers to take part in the business of displaying private fantasies on the market: it transforms the rebels into hirelings of business. The commercial father figure does not disappear from the bedroom, he stays right there and with his wife encourages the fantasies of the boy. But the boy does not gain his woman, nor his freedom. Even his fantasies are written for him by father. Father can write these fantasies better than the boy can imagine them. He employs girls to act as substitutes for real people, girls who remain fantasy figures but surpass in their beauty and doings the wildest dreams of the boy. So even the fantasies and the dreams become secondhand and remote-controlled. Even the imagination is alienated and purchaseable from the manufacturers of dreams. But the mass manufacturers of dreams deny love and real relationships. Their dream products are strictly make-believe, insincere. They are impersonal fantasies about impersonal encounters where sensations are the only things that matter and the I–Thou relationship between two people is kept out of the picture. Sexual experience is reduced to nothing but sensations.

The commercial advocates of the alternative community are not concerned with love and the complexities of attraction but with the titillation of the erotogenic zones, the ejaculation, the orgasm, in an entirely impersonal manner. Sexual experience becomes objectified into a thing – a thing to be sold and a thing to be had. It is no wonder that new sexual commodities have to be invented all the time. The store of human perversion has to be ransacked to create new stimuli and new commodities for sale. The merchants persuade the customers that like any other commodity the sex commodity enhances pleasure and in fact is superior to the pleasures provided by nature. We have already seen 'Judy' – the instant girlfriend – compared with whom "humans appear almost robotic."

There are about a dozen sex magazines on the market besides the handbooks, all devoted to sexual stimulation and the sale of sex goods. *Mayfair is* what may be called a better-class magazine of this type, being well-produced and modelling itself closely on *Penthouse* in layout and production technique. It has a feature on books, films, records and London night life. There are the usual pages of readers' letters exposing their erotic fantasies and adventures. Quite a few of these letters are from women, apparently from the middle-class. There is a special feature entitled 'Quest: A Laboratory of Human Responses' which consists of a series of interviews. This is a type of feature which under the guise of scientific investigation provides pornographic stimulation. It may be said that this is not all that unusual, as interest in the sexual and even medical sciences may be motivated by sexual curiosity, and the hidden search for titillation; a study of Stekel, Reich, etc., may arouse a certain sexual excitement in some readers. But these researchers were concerned with the sexual problems of human beings, their health and their character formations. The interviews in this feature

9. THE JOURNALISM OF PORNOGRAPHY

concentrate entirely on sexual performances and sexual situations, and do not allow the personality of their subjects to obtrude. In this journal as well as in others of this type, the emphasis is upon the sexually demanding woman, and male readers see themselves to a great extent as her object. The sexual powers of women, their capability of having repeated orgasms and of having sex with a number of men – sometimes one after the other – in order to obtain full gratification is a particular source of excitement to readers of these journals.

There is an American magazine called *Modern Man* which is more brash and outspoken in the modern American manner. The demanding attitude of the female is even more strongly stressed here: the woman as a lusting female, as a sex bomb, and the woman who needs the electric vibrator to give her proper satisfaction, the male's natural equipment and aptitude not being adequate for her satisfaction. How can a man's natural instincts and equipment suffice to satisfy a woman? The answer to the riddle of female gratification has only just been discovered: the electrical gadget – the technological penis. In the battle between man and technology the latter proves infinitely more effective and alive, even in the most natural and intimate of all human functions. Or is one to assume that the whole build-up is merely a publicity stunt of some entrepreneur out to make a quick fortune? Each way, the trend here is towards the image of the sexually demanding woman, and the man anxious to keep up with her must invoke the aid of the technological daddy to avoid humiliation and rejection.

To round up our exploration of the journalistic mirrors of 'liberated sex', we shall look at an English journal called *Probe*. This journal is possibly the most 'advanced' and a keen proselytiser of the new freedom. We find articles such as: 'The Astounding Sex-Life Of The Formerly Married'; 'Can Lib Lead To Les?'; 'Dr. Lesco Interviews Sexual Swoppers.' An article entitled: 'The New Sexual Demands Of Liberated Woman' looks like giving straightforward enlightenment to the big question of the effect of the sexual revolution upon women:

"So our society is changing fast: *Our mental totem poles are falling down, and as a consequence, women as well as men are developing sexual perversions* – and are probably better able to sustain them."

"The most prevalent demand was an inversion on the time worn attitude of women to sex-reluctance. Girls now seem to adore to be seduced, fingered, caressed, apparently without objection; in fact, with secret delight. Possibly this has always been so, but among the girls who were interviewed, it has become acknowledged openly. By dress and behaviour they deliberately encourage the exploring finger."

"Men are no longer the initiators and dominators in sex; they never were in fact, but a male-controlled society thought and behaved as if they were. Now the women call the tune and men have to dance to it. When the woman barrister appeared in our courts, the first female engineer designed a production line, the first woman airline pilot pushed the stick forward, the age-old top man was thrust into inferiority."

The highlight of woman's liberation as described in this article is the scene of one woman having intercourse with four men at the same time, exhausting them all and having orgasm after orgasm. "It gives me a wonderful feeling of power to know I have drained half-a-dozen men and could still take more." Here we have the image of Lilith in the guise of the liberated woman fantasy. One article entitled: 'It used to be Cheesecake for the Boys – Now it's Beefcake for the Girls':

"It has long been a truism of sexual research that men were more easily excited by photographs while the written word had a comparatively greater effect on women. This situation appears to have been changing and it looks like male pin-ups for the girls are on their way."

The article gives examples of women being sexually excited by pictures of nude men as well as descriptions of various types of sexual relationships, and shows a photograph of a girl masturbating as she looks at the male nude in *Cosmopolitan*. No doubt the article also serves to broaden the scope of the pornographers

9. THE JOURNALISM OF PORNOGRAPHY

by promoting the interests of an increasing number of liberated women voyeurs: "It is an inevitable and healthy part of Women's Lib that girlie magazines should be followed by Fella magazines."

The advertisements in this magazine are purely for sexual commodities and include the 'electric condom': the latest weapon in love's arsenal. Love eggs: 'used purely for women's private and personal pleasure wherever she is and whatever she is doing. Made of high quality non-toxic plastic. £3.50.' There is the ubiquitous personal vibrator, and the penis developer, which is designed for men who wish to increase the size of their erection. 'Vibrant sex power,' which is a kind of harness: 'vibrant sex power for every man. Multiple orgasm at will for every woman – the natural way! You hardly know you are wearing it until you switch on, then wow!' A totally different way of making love. £16.00. The imagery of rebellion against established morality is well expressed in the letters in this magazine:

" ... my passionate desire to seduce or be seduced by such females as would normally pass as respectable, married, widowed or otherwise short of opportunities to indulge in the tasting of forbidden fruits; it is the challenge to destroy the façade of a placid life and reduce them to a state of animal behaviour, the thought that to indulge in forbidden activities with a wife, preferably middle-aged and in other ways devoted to her husband, that has always given me the greatest excitement. What greater desire than to enter the home of a happily married couple after he has left for work and, under some pretext of selling some silly commodity or other, suddenly pull out ... no, wait for it, not what you think! Pull out of one's briefcase, quite by accident, a couple of photographs of oneself in the nude, at the back of which is written 'Ready for anything' or a similarly suggestive slogan ...

Such gambits have always been worth the trouble and the fact that the whole thing was done in an atmosphere of a remote danger that the rightful owner of your plaything might suddenly and unexpectedly return, only adds spice to the situation." [1]

This letter illustrates the exhibitionist's revenge against the superego and its norms, and his excitement in defying it. I was particularly impressed with the sentence from an earlier extract quoted in our italics, above: "Our mental totem poles are falling down and, as a consequence, women as well as men are developing sexual perversions."

It did not take the editors of *Penthouse* long to realise that there are a considerable number of people who want to write about their sexual problems and fantasies and see them published, and who also enjoy reading about other people's sexual preoccupations. Being good American businessmen the editors formulated a policy to provide a rationale for such a journal: "The sharing of sexual experiences about which many people have had feelings of guilt and shame has a beneficial cathartic effect. *Forum* is meant to function as a therapeutic vehicle in which readers can air their problems and receive expert advice."

Various encounter groups have sprung up in America and in Britain, devoted to body contact and body awareness and *Penthouse* and *Forum* not only encouraged them but had a hand in their organisation.

The editorial of the January 1973 issue of *Forum* declares: "We are a magazine that believes it has an important role to play in helping people in today's sexual society and therefore it is important to us not only in terms of finance but in terms of fulfilling our mission to catch the eye of new readers." The correspondence columns contain letters describing virtually every known deviation. Many of these letters are answered or enlarged upon by a team of consultants.

One recent issue contained an article entitled: 'Dr. Shepard's two-week turn-on' by Dr. Martin Shepard. This outlines a method of improving sensual and sexual awareness without drugs or mechanical gadgetry but by the interaction of two people helping each other to become aware of their bodies by massage and mutual bathing. This article reflects the ideas of the Esalen Institute in Big Sur, California, and shows how some fundamentally right concepts, that of arousing a wide range of body sensations in the relationship between two people, become perverted by a formalised regimen that forbids spontaneity. It promotes a

9. THE JOURNALISM OF PORNOGRAPHY

passive type of unisex where the different responses and needs of two people are obliterated by a methodical, alienated course of sensitisation. To train puritans in sexual responsiveness you subject them to a pedantic method of stimulations!

The expansion of the fantasy communication market has led to a proliferation of these handbooks and there are now about ten of them on the market, some of them short-lived. Among these we find: *In Depth, Janus, Search, Intra, Experience, Wide Open, His and Hers, Adult Advertiser*, etc. Only some of these contact magazines publish articles. It is interesting to observe that the articles printed are almost exclusively concerned with perversions such as fetishism, spanking, sadism and masochism, orgasm without a partner, that is by means of artificial sex aids, and so on. We can see a further regression of emotional and intellectual standards as even letter-writing is replaced in a number of these publications by advertisements by men and women, homosexual or heterosexual, normal or perverse, who either offer, or require, a service of some kind. The decline of articulation to mere advertisements is remarkable, but it illustrates the mental shrinking process that goes with pornographic infantilism. Even fantasies are restricted in many of these magazines to no more than collections of advertisements by perverse people trying to contact others, and for sex goods to help them in their activities.

There are also 'specialist journals' for homosexuals, transvestites, Lesbians, fetishists, and so on. Couples who wish to experiment with group sex and mate swopping with a number of different partners have to rely largely upon these contact magazines. The wide range of perversions shown in these magazines is not of course a new phenomenon – they are manifestations of deep-seated human sexual repression characteristic of patriarchal man. What is new is the publicity conferred upon these aberrations, their journalistic encouragement and commercial exploitation on a large scale.

1. *Probe Vol. 2, No. 1.*

10. Political Pornography

The main journals of political pornography (or the so-called underground press) are *It* and *Suck* (with *Oz* now defunct) and there are similar publications in America, often with a short life span. The significance of these papers is that they consider the sexual revolution to be a vehicle for the coming social revolution and, in this way, manage to bring together a wide spectrum of left wing opposition ranging from communists to anarchists, Maoists, Trotskyites, hippies, yippies, women's lib, drug addicts, psychedelists and mystics of all kinds. They are all against the established order, against the morality of capitalism, the family, the father, the domineering male, the old generation, the lackeys and the "pigs". They rebel against the property system, against work, against exploitation, against sexual taboos and any kind of social repression. The similarity between some of their statements (insofar as they manage to be coherent) and Wilhelm Reich's main dicta, is striking. No doubt many of these activists have heard about the more obvious ideas of Reich and, in particular, his concept of sex economy and sex politics. To quote from Reich:

> "Let us briefly summarise the sex-economic concepts of the relationship between human psychology and socio-economic factors. Society forms, alters and suppresses human needs; in this process, human structure is formed. This structure is not inborn, but develops in each individual in the course of the struggle between need and society. There is no congenital structure of the impulses; this structure is acquired in the course of the first few years of life. What is congenital is merely a larger or smaller amount of biological energy. Sexual suppression creates the structure of the serf who

10. POLITICAL PORNOGRAPHY

obeys and rebels at one and the same time. Today we want to produce 'free' people. Therefore we will have to know not only how the structure of the authoritarian individual was brought about, but what forces must be utilised in order to create a free structure. Since the core of psychic functioning is the sexual function, the core of practical psychology can be nothing but sexual politics." [1]

Compare this with Richard Neville (formerly the editor of *Oz*):

"Sexual repression and political repression were part of the same tradition and therefore the post-pubertal child should regard any voluntary sexual relationship as freedom and therapeutic ... the destruction of all inhibition is our aim."

Let us look at this notion of liberation by means of the destruction, denial and defiance of all inhibition.

Their struggle for the alternative society hinges upon the steadfast refusal to be repressed or influenced by the demands of bourgeois society. To break norms by violence or non-co-operation, by a refusal to accept any of the obligations imposed by the existing order, is the fundamental credo which unites most of the elements of the 'counter-culture'. What is missing here is an awareness of Reich's definition of repression, according to which the authoritarian morality is anchored in the character structure and the somatic armour of individuals. Understanding of the function of the armouring of the character structure in man is fundamental (according to Reich) to a cure of sick humanity and the overcoming of an irrational political system. This takes time and even the most fanatical Reichians admit this. But the underground, and the alternative society, do not have time. The change must come now in this generation, while we are still young, before the nuclear Armageddon makes nonsense of everything. So they use the grand weapon which Reich has discovered, namely the frustrated sexual yearning of the masses, in order to bring down the establishment which cannot exist without the sexual repression of men, women and children. To be sexually free is considered a death blow to the capitalist establishment.

But what happens if people with an armoured character structure adopt a posture of complete sexual freedom? Not having the time, ability or opportunity to free themselves from their internalised taboos and inhibitions, they will use their sexuality as a weapon to defeat the superego. In doing so their sexuality acquires aggressive characteristics; they will associate sexuality with aggression. The more they fuck and the more they repeat the word fuck, the more they imagine that they hurt and will defeat the system. As they consider themselves a sexually repressed class which is in the process of acquiring its freedom, they call upon all sexually repressed people to overthrow the system by fucking as much as they want to. The emphasis is upon the destruction of the system and the libido becomes more and more sadistic. Or rather let us say that they regress to the sadistic level in sexuality and in political activity. Sexual and political aggressiveness is equated with the fight for freedom.

The magazine *Oz* perfectly illustrated the phantasmagoria of sadism. There were a great number of drawings and pictures of an indescribable sadistic nature, depicting human bodies being torn to pieces or disembowelled, often accompanied by sexual activities, all in lurid technicolour. Drawings of people unspeakably deformed were quite commonplace. Necrophilia was presented as an entertaining pastime and one article, in the form of a satire on necrophilia, went into all the details: "I talk to my dead lovers quite often and, of course, we never have trouble with ego-shrinking complaints about your abilities. A corpse will never mock you and they never get tired. You have them satisfied every time." This is a more innocuous passage from the article. Maybe some of it is funny, but that certainly cannot be said of the drawings. Necrophilia has the attraction of sexual fulfilment with a person who has already been killed, i.e. whose resistances have been destroyed. An extraordinary double-page photograph, obviously a montage, depicted dozens of dead bodies standing propped against the walls of a large corridor and two young people standing in the middle talking together and quite unmoved at the horror around them. An advert for a film entitled 'Love and Murder in the Commune' had this to recommend it: "The unbelievable manifesto of the assassin cult – worship him, kill for him, die for him, make love for him."

10. POLITICAL PORNOGRAPHY

Even the astrological charts of *Oz*, called Oztrology, managed to acquire a sadistic character with the various signs of the Zodiac suitably depicted as snake's fangs attacking something, a heart pierced by daggers, a skull with prominent teeth and a swastika. There was a feature reporting the activities of the counter-culture. The title drawing of this feature depicts a spike upon which four human figures are impaled. It contains one item entitled: 'It's all in the blood – the vampire freaks':

> "Some young gentlemen of our acquaintance, having a needle habit, were forced at the heaviest stage of their addiction to economise on food, and existed frugally on *Nestles Milk* and *Ambrosia Creamed Rice*. As a supplement they had a brilliant idea. Every time a friend came to jack up in their flat, they levied a toll of a works-full of blood (2mls) which was then emptied into a large green Tupperware bowl in the kitchen. Come Sunday night, their flat being something of a shooting gallery, the bowl would be full, and the contents transferred to a double boiler saucepan."

There were strip cartoons in every issue. One was entitled 'Inter-City Romance' and concerned the sexual adventures of a young drug addict whose efforts at intercourse are repeatedly interrupted by his hallucinations, much to the disgust and frustration of his coloured girl friend. There is much wham, bang and things exploding, rows of phalluses and vaginas in extraordinary distortions.

The sexual fantasies of a revolutionary who wants to destroy in order to liberate himself become sadistic. He wants to free his incarcerated libido by blowing up the armour of his own body, by making himself explode and also the environment in which he exists. He wants to tear the armour, the restrictions, the internalised symbols of law and order from himself in order to be free. Sadism in the service of liberation of the libido is one of the most basic manifestations of deprived and inhibited men. We have seen it operating among the romantics, and we see it here depicted in a brutal de-sublimated manner: the rage of the repressed who wants to smash the prison walls of inhibitions.

Besides the sadistic character of many features and drawings we can also notice a wide range of anal aggressive manifestations in this journal. There were drawings of a particularly burly young woman who was in the habit of expelling her faeces forcefully into the face of her young lover.

All the articles had a highly sarcastic and deprecatory tone which went beyond muckraking. The cult of deprecation was applied even to themselves and in the January 1973 issue we find Richard Neville reflecting on his fate in an article entitled: 'All Dressed Up and Nowhere to Go'. He was introduced on the title page:

> "Richard Neville, revolutionary *bon viveur* and gadfly of the *Oz* editorial collective, pens his annual state of the nation message and wonders, as he drifts in ever-decreasing circles around the backwaters of his mind, whether we can harness our presently dissipated energies and rescue ourselves from our self-created cultural and political myths. It seems so shallow to occasionally pick up the gauntlet of the State with a flourish of plagiarised slogans or to fight a journalistic revolution upon a barricade of underground press cards ..."

Another important characteristic which could be taken as intellectual dishonesty is, in fact, a symptom of dissociation. Contradictory statements are made on all sorts of issues and the nonsensicality, the lack of logic and cohesion, is not even hidden but paraded almost as a virtue. It is indeed the babbling of angry infants who know that they can't think clearly but that this is perfectly OK because clear and logical thinking is part of the ammunition of the grown-up world. Reason and logic are felt to be a prison which keeps spontaneity locked up. And as these youngsters do have to think sometimes (when their strip-cartoons, drugs, pop sounds or sex are not available), then they will think in their own way. They feel that the real world, in which responsible or coherent thought appears, is the enemy in any case and do not wish to be associated with it. So they use infantile incoherence as their particular way of being themselves.

Another aspect of the new freedom is the emergence of woman

10. POLITICAL PORNOGRAPHY

not merely as a unisex creature who "also has sexual urges" but as the powerful goddess who dominates man and, by doing so, defeats the male world and its rules and taboos. The alternative culture invokes female power to break down the establishment of males, and the more she shows her power and aggression the better for all. 'La belle dame sans merci' is not depicted in lyrical verse but as wielding weapons, raping males, and above all by a great show of vagina dentatas, i.e. vaginas with teeth.

Another journal of this type is *IT*, short for 'International Times', which appears to be more politically orientated. It certainly veers towards some queer kind of Maoism and the issue of January 1973 has smiling Mao on its front page, and a letter from Mao inside with yet another picture of smiling Mao. The trend towards supporting the 'other' superego to break down or defeat their own superego is more emphasised here: while everything in the capitalist system needs to be busted up and all its financial, political, juridical and scientific strangleholds upon people's freedom destroyed, the others, as represented by Maoist China, North Vietnam, Black Panther, Anarchists and Trotskyites must be supported.

Political and sexual discontent is used methodically and cynically to create an atmosphere of rebelliousness on an even lower level than in *Oz*, where there was at least occasional self-questioning. There are the usual adverts for pornographic literature, sex aids, and many small ads offering 'personal services'.

There is no doubt that left-wing organisations exploit the sex-orientated trend of these journals for their own ends, and use the sexual discontent of young people and their overt hostility towards the establishment as a means to weaken capitalism and to serve their own aspirations. In the long run, however, they will do themselves little good with this policy for they will themselves have to fight against these dissociative and regressive trends in order not to be confined to the fantasy rebellions of an infantilistic cult. In fact there is already a counter-attack among the politically orientated against the mock-rebellions which go on in the heads and genitals of the sexual underground.

1. Wilhelm Reich: *The Sexual Revolution* (Vision Press, 1961).

11. The Sex-Mechanics

We have seen how a commercial and pseudo-revolutionary sexual liberation promotes a depersonalised and regressive sexuality, leaving the fundamental, unconscious repressions intact.

The ego, confronted by the demands of sexual freedom, can repress sexuality and dissociate itself from it in yet another way: it can project sexuality into the outside world and see it as an object. Sexual desire itself is placed outside the ego and seen 'objectively', for the purposes of scientific investigation. The impression of sexual freedom can be obtained through unrestricted and impersonal scientific observation. When the experience of subjectivity, the inner sense of being alive, when the communication of subjective feelings through love and friendship is not possible for the armoured and alienated man, he will either buy a sex symbol or commodity or he will make a scientific research project to measure human reactions, to discover in this way what he cannot know subjectively.

When many intelligent people were aware of the importance of sex as an aetiological and causative factor in all kinds of behavioural and emotional aberrations, science soon felt it incumbent upon itself to subject the sex drive to scientific observation and analysis. Now, it is one of the most difficult and puzzling problems of the philosophy of science to know how the inner drives of man, his emotions, fantasies, goals and desires can be studied scientifically, that is to say, objectively; how a science of psychology is possible at all and how the processes that are internal to man can be seen outside himself as objects suitable for quantitative observation.

Scientific objectivity, after its successes in the physical sciences, has applied itself to the psycho-social sciences with only

11. THE SEX-MECHANICS

questionable success. The assumption is that where there is a mind, or drive or energy, there must be action or reaction; where there is stimulus from inside or outside there must be an observable response. The quantitative sciences do not even presume to deal with the internal experiences of mind or drive or emotions, only with their observable manifestations. The inner experiences of emotions, dreams, fantasies or ideas – all those things in fact which constitute personality – are not suitable data for the objective sciences.

So far so good! But many scientists transform a methodological limitation into a universal principle which declares that mind and inner feelings, not being observable by the scientific method, are of no significance. They subject psycho-biological processes to physicalistic models. The former, however, operate in a different way from the latter and it is a kind of rape to subject the psychological or emotional to the mechanistic models that operate in physics. It is the reductionism of the 'nothing but' kind, of which Viktor Frankl has spoken, that has so impoverished and disfigured the psycho-biological sciences. Man's alienation from himself, from the uniqueness of his being, is manifested in a science that approaches him as an object, as an outside being, measuring and controlling him as a thing. The man who has been depersonalised no longer places his experiences inside himself but outside himself. The science of sex will be for him one form of contact with sexuality which he cannot experience fully in himself.

Ivan Pavlov, the father of the conditioned reflex theory, constantly reiterated that he was a physiologist, and that he was concerned with the observation of reflexes of animals under certain artificially established conditions from which, by induction, he made some careful and limited generalisations about human behaviour. He did not consider himself to be a psychologist and repeatedly stressed that the field of internal experiences, approachable only, as he thought, by introspection, were not his province. But we have seen how, out of the work of this man of high integrity and intelligence, a cult emerged which attacked with considerable ferocity the psychology of 'internal experience', especially psychoanalysis.

Up to now the researchers of the physiology of sexual responses have not shown this kind of hostility – their terms of reference are much more succinct and well-defined than those of the behaviourists. But confusion arises when those who are hostile or defensive towards psychoanalysis generalise their findings and establish them as a system of the 'nothing but' kind. Existentialist psychologists, on the other hand, feel very strongly about a laboratory-based sexology, for they claim that it destroys the wholeness of a human experience if it is analysed merely by the explicitness of its details. They rightly object that the computation of a great number of details does not make a whole, and that little evidence can be had about the state of a person by collating a large number of his measurable reflexes or responses. I think that this objection is valid.

One of the important aspects of depersonalised or dissociated sex is that it is preoccupied with part objects. The erotic zones become separated from the personality, and the whole process of love, affection and desire is reduced to the preoccupation with genitals and other erotogenic zones. Under the impact of this process we do not say, this is her vagina or her breast, her eyes, her hair, her skin, her smell, her mind, her body, her voice, her conversation, and therefore I love her or am excited by her, and I want to be loved and desired by her because I am a whole person also, with a mind, a will that means something and a body that feels; we rather say that there is a vulva, a vagina, a pair of legs which excite me; her thoughts and her mind have nothing to do with the physical organs that excite me.

The scientist who is concerned with the study of sexual functions will be concerned with the measurable processes of the genitals, the heart-beat, the respiration, secretions and orgastic discharge which he can measure thanks to scientific technology. He looks at human beings in their most intimate responses as part objects, he isolates the genital and physiological functions from the personality, from the inner experience of a person. He is alienated from the persons whom he observes, even as he is alienated from his own libido in the process of observation. He sees an experience merely from outside. He is not concerned with subjective factors, but he can measure the excitements of the penis, the clitoris, the nipples, the engorgement of blood vessels, the swelling of the labia majora and the labia minora and the vaginal walls. In the observation of these data he assumes that he can observe and measure sexual excitement in human beings.

In their book *Human Sexual Response*, Dr Masters and Mrs Johnson of the 'Reproductive Biology Research Foundation' in St. Louis, report on their ten years of investigation in which they have observed more than ten thousand male and female orgasms, and how the human body responds to erotic stimulation during both masturbation and coitus. Responses of the penis, scrotum and testes, the breasts, clitoris, labia, vagina, cervix, uterus and other parts of the body are all presented and explained. The Masters and Johnson study made it possible to follow the entire human sexual cycle from the first stirrings of erotic desire through orgasm to ultimate subsidence, as objectively as nineteenth century physiologists had followed the digestive cycle from mastication to excretion.

The excitement stage is the first of four successive levels or phases which they have observed in the cycle of human sexual response. The second stage is the plateau phase, then the orgasm and lastly resolution. In the plateau stage the man's testes increase in diameter by about fifty percent over their unstimulated size and are pulled up into the scrotum, the rate of breathing increases and there is a further increase in pulse rate and blood pressure. A few drops of moisture may emerge from the Bartholin's glands embedded in the labia majora, as well as from the male urethra. The most dramatic change in women during the plateau phase, as Masters and Johnson found out, is the engorgement and swelling of tissue surrounding the outer third of the vagina. The diameter of the outer third of the vagina is reduced by as much as fifty percent actually gripping the penis. In the orgasm stage there is a series of rhythmic contractions of the upper third of the vaginal barrel, from three to six such muscular contractions taking place. In the male there are similar contractions, lasting about four-fifths of a second, during which ejaculation takes place. Pulse rate, blood pressure and breathing rate reach a peak. During the resolution phase, which is analogous to Reich's "pleasant body and psychic relaxation," Masters and Johnson observe an immediate return to normal of the areolas surrounding the nipples, a rapid disappearance of the sex flush, the clitoris returns to its unstimulated position, the outer third of the vagina increases in diameter. In men there is the prompt loss of erection of the penis and its shrinking back to its unstimulated size. In both men and women the pulse rate, blood pressure and breathing rate gradually return to normal.

These are some of the empirical observations made by Masters and Johnson on 382 women and 312 men during more than ten thousand cycles of sexual orgasm and return to an unexcited state:

> "These observations were made not only during masturbation and intercourse, but also during artificial coition – a laboratory procedure that makes accessible to direct vision and to recording on motion picture film internal changes observable in no other way." [1]

If one reads the report one cannot fail to be impressed by the meticulousness and efficiency with which they approached and carried out their research. It is true that a number of revealing physiological responses were obtained that were not available before, and it is most gratifying to a psychoanalyst and in particular one who upholds many of Reich's theories, that most of these findings support both Freud's and Reich's much earlier formulations. Furthermore the psychoanalytic theory of sexual energy discharge through orgasm and its physiological rhythms of excitement – tension, orgastic discharge, relaxation – are verified in these observations. Particularly interesting from a Reichian point of view are their observations with prostitutes, who very often suffer from pelvic congestion, due to the fact that after repeated intercourse in which they experience stimulation, they do not obtain orgastic release. One of the most important areas of muscular rigidity which relates to orgastic impotence is, in Reich's view, the pelvic region. The rigidity of the armoured pelvis makes full orgastic experience difficult and is, at the same time, the result of inhibition. Pelvic rigidity, together with tense abdominal walls, are the most important areas which impede free sexual mobility.

11. THE SEX-MECHANICS

In 1949 Dr. Howard C. Taylor, one of America's foremost gynaecologists, stated that a number of gynaecological problems were related to chronic pelvic congestion, the chronic engorgement of blood vessels in the uterus and associated pelvic organs, and suggested that the whole congestion fibrosis syndrome was traceable, at least in some cases, to a constantly recurring pattern of experiencing sexual arousal without orgasmic release. Masters and Johnson found in their observations dramatic verification of this process. Reich's concept of armouring is not quite the same, as it is concerned with chronic contraction of the musculature due to unconscious inhibition and refusal to allow sexual convulsions to take place. No doubt we can say that the unconscious inhibitions and muscular rigidities precede pelvic congestion and cause it, insofar as they do not permit full orgastic release. Nevertheless, the incidence of pelvic congestion as a result of absence of orgastic release is a corollary to Reich's theoretical model.

Let us compare Reich's way of describing the four stages with that of Masters and Johnson. Let us start with the phase of involuntary muscle contraction which Masters and Johnson called the orgasmic platform of the plateau, or phase two, during which, as we saw, the diameter of the upper part of the vagina contracts by fifty percent. Reich calls this the phase of involuntary muscle contractions:

> "The increase in excitation can no longer be controlled voluntarily, while it takes hold of the whole personality and produces tachycardia and deep expiration. Bodily excitement becomes more and more concentrated upon the genitals, a melting kind of sensation sets in, which may best be described as a radiation of excitation from the genitals to other parts of the body. This excitation results first in involuntary contractions of the total musculature of the genitals and of the pelvic floor. These contractions occur in waves. The crests of the waves occur with the complete penetration of the penis, the troughs with the retraction of the penis. However as soon as the retractions go beyond a certain limit there occur immediate spasmodic contractions which expedite

ejaculation. In the woman there occurs in this case a contraction of the smooth musculature of the vagina." [2]

These descriptions coincide closely with the observations of Masters and Johnson, but compare the difference in the language. One is the description, albeit scientific, of an experience, the other of a series of objective events. The one is something that can be seen to happen to a human person, the other is a series of physical data in which the personal aspect is unrecognisable and irrelevant. We see the contrasts more emphatically in the next stage as described by Reich:

> "The orgastic excitation takes hold of the whole body musculature ... what we call the release of tension is predominantly the result of a flowing back of the excitation from the genitals to the body. This flowing back is experienced as a sudden decrease of the tension. After acme the complete flowing back of the excitation towards the whole body is what constitutes gratification. Before the zero point is reached, the excitation tapers off in a gentle curve and is replaced by *a pleasant bodily and psychic relaxation*. The sensual relations have subsided; what continues is a grateful, tender attitude towards the partner."

And he sums up:

> "Looking back over the two main phases of the sexual act we see that the first phase is characterised mainly by the sensory, the second phase by the motor experience of pleasure." [3]

We see that these observations relate not only to a human or personal experience but to the pleasure experienced at the various stages of sexual excitement and the satisfaction that comes with relaxation. Pleasure and satisfaction are indeed the most important aspects of the orgastic discharge. The capacity of experiencing deep pleasure indicates discharge capacity, while in the pathological person pleasure anxiety and orgasm anxiety go

11. THE SEX-MECHANICS

together to produce that inability for discharge, that condition of sexual stasis, that creates not only a congested pelvis but a whole host of neurotic conditions so characteristic of inhibited man of patriarchy. Reich says that the involuntary contractions of the organism and the complete discharge of the excitation are the most important criteria of orgastic potency, which he differentiates from erectile and ejaculative capacity which can occur without full orgasm. "Clinical experience has shown that man, as a result of the general sexual repression, has lost the capacity for ultimate sexual surrender."

Reich is deeply concerned with the unconscious psychological inhibitions characteristic of patriarchal man and the somatic tensions which accompany it. He describes the physiological manifestations observed, in terms of pleasure, surrender and relaxation, as a personal subjective experience in the act of sexuality. In the whole report of Masters and Johnson such personal terms are not employed. One can read the detailed descriptions of physiological responses of 694 people during more than 10,000 cycles of sexual excitation, and not know that they are individuals, persons who feel, think, have pleasure or pain; they are depicted as bodies undergoing certain reflexes with not a mind between them. They are things observed in action, objective occurrences. In other words the physical responses are dissociated from the ego of the person that experiences and *has* these bodily responses. It is interesting to study the detailed descriptions of Masters and Johnson of the resolution phase. This makes one wonder how many of them had full orgasm in Reichian terms.

We are not acknowledged as persons in sex; our sexual ego, our sexual self-consciousness is ignored and only a biological and mechanical function remains, described in great scientific detail, to be sure, but still impersonal. And here we have the problem. However detailed the studies of Masters and Johnson and their plans to overcome impediments in proper sexual, orgastic functioning, the primary repression remains if the personality, the 'I' that feels and desires, is not acknowledged. For real gratification in sex is personal, the sense of a unique personal experience that embraces the whole self. We can also say that the narcissistic dimension plays a great part in sexuality which, if satisfied, can acknowledge the narcissism, the self-feeling, of the other. For he who cannot love himself cannot love another. The negation of the personality dimension in the mechanistic sex view is a kind of narcissistic castration. If the love for oneself is denied then we cannot love and respect the sexual partner. I and she, I and thou, becomes reduced then to 'It' and 'It': two impersonal objects functioning outside themselves. This is not only culturally deplorable but is clinically malignant, for it perpetuates the inhibition and armour which has been created in our culture.

Consciousness as well as pleasure are important channels of energy discharge, and if this discharge of energy into consciousness and pleasure is blocked we remain fundamentally impotent. Sexual discharge will be a part discharge and the full surrender to pleasure will be absent. However efficient the biological mechanical orgasm reflex may be, it cannot be a complete discharge of excitement, for the excitement of the mind and of self-consciousness in the relationship between the sexes, the sense of being accepted and of being loved, is a fundamental requisite of happiness. Without the capacity for happiness we shall remain frustrated, disappointed, mistrustful and angry; we cannot love ourselves nor can we love others. To paraphrase the situation: in the past sex was negated, now sex is free and our ego is negated. It amounts to the same thing in terms of fundamental inhibitions.

Masters and Johnson began to realise the psychological factors during their therapeutic investigations. They became aware of the disastrous effects of sexual repression – "sexual puritanism and Victorianism" – upon orgastic performance. Their 'Reproductive Biology Research Foundation' is now devoted to an investigation of psychological as well as physiological causes of sexual malfunctioning. There is no therapist, however behaviouristically or physiologically orientated he may be, who does not realise sooner or later that psychological factors, often stemming from childhood, are at the root of behavioural or sexual pathologies. But their concept of psychology is often so narrow that they have to rely largely on physiological conditioning in therapy.

Let me quote the concluding passage from E. M. Brecher's book, *The Sex Researchers*, which illustrates the problem of in-

11. THE SEX-MECHANICS

telligent scientists trapped in the limitations which objectivism has created for them:

> "When I began work on this book three years ago, I had a vague feeling that sexual inhibitions and frustrations have effects far broader than are realised – that some of the bigotry, hostility and strife which characterise our era might have deep sexual roots. I hoped that a release from feelings of sexual guilt and shame might lead to warmer, richer interpersonal relationships – and to a relaxation of the tensions which are threatening to rend our society, perhaps to destroy mankind. A healthy society requires healthy people; perhaps, I thought, sexual fulfilment is one of the preconditions of human health."

These feelings about the effects of sexual inhibition in terms of hostility and aggression led Theodor Reik, Otto Fenichel, Karl Abraham and, above all, Wilhelm Reich to investigate the correlations between sexual repression and aggression. They discovered the sexual roots in a number of aberrations of human behaviour, including sadism, aggression and paranoia.

Freud in his early work discovered the sexual basis of neuroticism and aggressiveness, but his early therapeutic formulation that many neurotic symptoms representing blocked sexual energy would disappear if sexual energy were set free (in other words if it could obtain orgastic release in intercourse) was contradicted. Neurotic symptoms or even neurasthenic conditions often failed to disappear with orgastic discharge. Reich, who upheld the fundamental correctness of Freud's definition of neurosis, was puzzled by these failures and this led him into a detailed analysis of the orgastic function. In the course of this he found that only full orgastic potency, as differentiated from blocked, armoured or partial orgasm, would provide the deep fulfilment and sexual release which eliminates neurotic or aggressive impulses. He found, as indeed the common sense and experience of people knew for a long time, that there is orgasm and orgasm; that there is a great deal of difference between an orgasm snatched with personal indifference or an orgasm experienced with a deep sense of fulfilment. Furthermore there is a difference in the sexual experience between an anxious or neurotic person and that of a happy loving one. He found that this was not only a question of psychic attitudes but also one of physical tensions which are often not fully released in the orgastic reflex.

The idea fostered by Masters and Johnson that all orgasms are alike (the only difference being the number of orgasms that a woman may experience in intercourse or masturbation) was largely based upon the concept of the difference between sensory experience and motor experience, the distinction between the sensation and stimulation and involuntary motor discharge. Involuntary discharge, being a motor reflex, is considered the same in all cases. This is not correct. The motor discharge does, in fact, show very considerable differences in people according to the amount of psychic inhibition and muscular rigidity which sets a limit to the full movement and bodily convulsions.

Their neglect or inability to study the subjective quality of an orgastic experience led Masters and Johnson into making an important mistake. What they consider multiple orgasm in women induced by the stimulation of the clitoris by means of masturbation, particularly by artificial vibrators, is usually no more than a series of orgasmic spasms which do not involve the whole body and often not even the vagina. These spasms, of which a woman can have many in quick succession, do not lead to a full discharge of tension, to the "pleasant bodily and psychic relaxation" that signifies an orgasm.

Orgasmic spasms without proper orgastic discharge are well known to sexologists and usually occur in women who suffer from sexual inhibitions and an inability to yield to orgastic release. They are often subject to domination-submission conflicts and associate vaginal yearnings and orgasm with submission and self-loss which they cannot tolerate. (I shall return to these problems in the next chapter.)

Many people preach and practise the greatest possible amount of sexual orgasm as a kind of panacea without realising that the removal of the superficial taboo against sexuality often leaves the

11. THE SEX-MECHANICS

deeper repressions intact, and the orgasm experienced is frequently only a restricted part discharge of the libido.

So, the notion that the achievement of physiological orgasm necessarily leads to health and well-being is erroneous, for it can perpetuate psychic and physiological blocks, unreleased energy that continues to manifest itself in aggression or anxiety. The argument about happiness from the physical premiss is, therefore, of limited significance in human beings and needs to be corrected if the sexual freedom which we are preaching is not to lead us into a blind alley.

1. An Analysis of *Human Sexual Response – Masters and Johnson*, edited by Ruth and Edward Brecher (André Deutsch, 1967).
2. Wilhelm Reich: *The Function of the Orgasm* (Farrar, Straus & Cudahy, 1961).
3. *Ibid.*

12. The Liberation of Women

H. G. Wells called the emancipation of women one of the most important events of the twentieth century. He realised in the 1920s that it would have an impact on society far greater than anyone imagined at the time.

Now fifty years later a second feminist wave seeks to go beyond the old demands for constitutional equality, which characterised the suffragette movement, towards woman's liberation from a great many sexual and social taboos. The approach to the 'woman question' is now much more far-reaching and radical, as the very foundations of male superiority are under attack.

While in patriarchal cultures men are subjected to sexual repression and guilt, women are subjected to men. With the onset of patriarchy during the agricultural revolution which had its beginnings in the natural wheat-growing areas of Palestine and Southern Turkey some ten thousand years ago, men began to dominate the household and the family; they became the domestic rulers, the economic providers in possession of the knowledge and the skills upon which agriculture depended. Women gradually assumed a subordinate role; they were deprived of spiritual and economic power, and the main responsibilities of decision-making passed from them. With the advent of monotheism all the female goddesses were ousted from the heavens and women no longer had a God. They became dependent upon the men who related themselves to God and who considered themselves his representatives on earth. The woman is concerned with God only through the man, she can serve God only by pleasing man: "He for God alone – she for God in him."[1] Of course she remains important; she is important for the purposes of man but in her importance she becomes a means, a symbol, an object. She is not an autonomous being but an object for man's erotic needs, his comforts, and for procreation. Her mind is not concerned with

12. THE LIBERATION OF WOMEN

higher things, with truth or law or with the will of God; God does not speak to her, only to man – she has to listen and obey. Even her body, her sexuality has become as passive-dependent upon man as her mind; she ceases to believe in the spontaneity and the demands of her sexual urges. Her body and her sexuality are considered the objects of man's needs and desires, and her role is to respond to him, to respond beautifully, with pleasure, but without an independent, authentic sexual urge, for that would make her a being in her own right and not subservient to the male. Without a mind sharpened by responsibility and broadened by knowledge, and deprived of her spirituality, she is helpless and dangerous – at the same time subservient and untamed.

In certain cultural variants of patriarchy the emphasis is upon female sensuality, upon the woman as a primitive being unspiritual and near to nature, a being that constantly threatens to draw man away from his higher purposes into the realm of lust, as amongst the Ancient Greeks and medieval Christians, and at other times the emphasis is upon her delicacy, her preciousness that needs to be protected from man's sensuous brutality. Actually the two apparent opposite concepts of femininity can go side by side in Christianity, insofar as Christianity upholds a dualistic concept of man, splitting him into a natural barbarian and a dessicated spirit, and this split is reflected in the Christian image of the woman.

Broadly speaking, however, the desexualisation of woman has greatly dominated Christian patriarchal thinking, and her natural self has been relegated to the fantasies of hell, temptation and lust from which both men and women must be saved by the intervention of God, Jesus and the Church. The important point in all this is to realise that women have ceased to project an image of themselves; they have ceased to project their own feminine self-image and exist only as an image created by man, as a certain being to whom he is constantly and fatally drawn, against whom he has to fight to preserve his own purity or alternatively has to protect from his lusts and brutalities.

Now, as patriarchal culture is faced with a crisis, women try to project their own self-image, to liberate themselves from the impositions of man's imagery of woman, towards the attainment of a feminine self-consciousness as authentic beings. Ben Jonson claimed that "women are but shadows of us men", and women begin to shout to the world that they want to emerge from this shadow.

Women have clearly borne the brunt of the repressive super-ego of patriarchy, and the freedom of women, their personal and sexual equality, must obviously play an essential role in any freedom movement. While men, conscious of the age-old barriers to sexual self-expression, demand the right to break the old taboos and inhibitions in order to be free to satisfy their sexual needs without opprobrium, women are beginning to claim the same rights. Anyone who supports the liberation of sexuality must support the liberation not only of female sexuality but of women as persons. Anyone who accepts and respects his sexuality accepts and respects the objects of his sexuality. In the case of man he respects, admires and loves women (generally speaking) and in the case of a woman she admires and loves men (generally speaking).

The struggle of women for self-respect and equality has however acquired an aggressiveness that is directed against men in general. The image of woman as passive and dependent, the self-negating madonna, and wife, gives way to an image of the angry woman who seeks revenge for centuries of subjugation. While previously the image of the revenging woman, the castrating Lilith, was the property of man's sado-masochistic imagination, now women tend to act out this fantasy themselves and the women's liberation activist has become not so much the activist for the freedom of female sexuality and dignity, but of the female rage and her hostility against man. This emphasis upon the secondary drives leads many women who are sexual deviationists to take a leading role in the struggle and turn it into a struggle for the freedom to be perverse. It is not a good thing that Lesbians consider themselves as the spokesmen for the freedom of women, and a women's liberation movement which emphasises aggression and vindictiveness will soon forget what freedom to be a woman is all about and will lead the revolution into a dead end.

Before this quite happens, let us see what goes on in the name

12. THE LIBERATION OF WOMEN

of women's liberation and examine some of its deviations. I have considerable sympathy for rebels who, surrounded by a wall of incomprehension and bad faith, vent their rage and attack a world that would not acknowledge their real needs. But because I am concerned with the real freedom of sexuality I am disturbed about a freedom struggle that promotes the freedom for aggression and loses sight of the freedom of femininity.

The new confusions and misrepresentations of the issues at stake, the phantasmagoria of hate that has begun to dominate the argument about freedom for women, would be pathetic or amusing were it not for the new repression of female sexuality which they entail.

The arguments against vaginal sexuality in favour of clitoral sexuality, the depicting of the male as a sadist and the female as the helpless masochist, the concept of women as an oppressed class who have to fight the dominant class of males, the overcompensatory emphasis upon the superiority of women, tend to obfuscate the real issue. I shall give some examples of these misplaced arguments and then try to draw attention to what I consider to be the real issue.

MAN THE ENEMY

Every social movement concerned with freedom for the oppressed had the emancipation of women high on its agenda. The fight against the bourgeois property system with its degradation of human relationships into master and serf, capitalist and worker, drew the exploited and oppressed classes together. The fight against the exploiters was not merely a fight for the redistribution of wealth but also against authoritarianism and the sense of personal oppression by a dominant class.

Women who had to bear the brunt of the sex-denying image of authoritarian society instinctively felt that freedom meant freedom to please and be pleased; freedom to make their own sexual choices and to enjoy their sexuality. It meant therefore the dignity of female sexuality, the dignity of women. The participation of women in the struggle against oppression gave them a full cultural and spiritual dimension. The God of freedom was their God as well as the God of their males, and in the fight for human equality female equality was naturally emphasised. The change of the economic base of society and the introduction of values alternative to the authoritarian values was regarded as the very essence of socialism as it was understood in Europe before and shortly after the First World War; it meant the emancipation of people, and women were people who participated in the fight. It was a fight against the social repressions that reproduced themselves in the individual, and it was a fight against individual repressions which reproduced themselves in society. In short, social revolution meant liberation of men and women from a repressive social and moral system.

Many revolutionaries and above all many intelligent women revolutionaries in Russia and Germany, women like Rosa Luxemburg and Madame Kollontai held that women's liberation could take place only as a result of the creation of a new social and economic system. Madame Kollontai, generally regarded as one of the most articulate and intelligent 'libertines' of the Russian revolution, put the aim of the social revolution with regard to the liberation of sexuality, beautifully in these words: "The task of the revolutionary working class is to create healthier and more joyous relations between the sexes."

We have seen how authoritarianism began to dominate the communist revolution in Russia and how, under Stalin, the gains of the revolution were gradually betrayed by a dictatorial bureaucracy that cared nothing for personal freedom and self-expression. One of the first victims of the authoritarian degeneration of the revolution was sexual freedom and in particular the sexual freedom of women. As Reich observed: "The repression of the movement towards a new sexual morality is the first symptom of betrayal of the revolution."

So the revolution was betrayed in one of its most important aspects and authoritarianism came back with a vengeance. Dictatorship in the name of communism, and capitalism in the name of democracy dominated the social and political field and after the Second World War patriarchal authoritarianism imposed itself unchallenged once more.

12. THE LIBERATION OF WOMEN

The struggle for women's liberation in these conditions remained on a superficial level. An individualistic and intellectualised aggressiveness replaced concern for fundamental social change. Women could not participate in a common struggle against the repressive base of society, when the real enemy, the authoritarian bourgeois system, was practically impervious to attack, and only an individualistic literary form of aggression seemed possible. Men, *sui generis*, became the representatives of female oppression. The argument turned into a personal attack upon men as sexual sadists who obtained their gratifications through domination over women.

An excellent example of this type of attack is presented by Kate Millett. Her attacks on patriarchy focus upon the "status category of sex" and she sees patriarchal politics as essentially sexual politics designed to consolidate male power.

We may consider this to be a grossly simplistic view of patriarchy, certainly a woman's view who considers female liberation as essentially liberation from man's dominance over her. Her approach is illustrated by her use of long extracts from the writings of Henry Miller, Norman Mailer and Genet, and she has no difficulty in showing that these men depict the sex act as an exercise of male power in its most ruthless and sadistic forms. Now if Kate Millett tries to show that these literary examples are typical male sexual attitudes she is either very naive or thoroughly disingenuous. We know that these writers present sexuality in a sadistic destructive form, bent upon asserting man's phallic power, woman's inability to resist it and her degradation in the satisfaction of the male. We also know that this sadistic streak had a considerable vogue in the cult of the American tough guy during and after the Second World War, with its emphasis upon the ruthless go-getter and adventurer.

Indeed, ruthlessness was presented as a desirable quality of American civilisation not only in books but in countless gangster and adventure films denying the manifestation of warm feelings as unmanly; any feelings that were allowed to be shown were sentimental kitsch reserved for the innocent girl from next door or the ubiquitous momma. It would be useful to enquire how much of this male characteristic was 'cultivated' by a bourgeoisie which propagated the virtues of unrestrained competition in the service of free enterprise. The commercial jungle would certainly encourage aggression; and women would be seen as commodities for gratification and things to be possessed. The anal appeal of this process is very important, as I have shown earlier, as it contributes towards the transformation of the living environment and the people in it into a number of things which do not need to be respected.

The passages Kate Millett quotes are indeed prime examples of sexual regression to phallic aggression and anal destruction, as well as necrophiliac fantasies. We have seen these perversions in the journals of commercial and political pornography where they are meant to outrage bourgeois respectability, destroy its values and 'serve the revolutionary struggle'.

We have seen the manifestations of Satanism in the romantic movement and have shown how defiance and aggression towards the moral values of a restrictive superego can lead to sadism, and phallic as well as anal aggression. We have seen that the armoured character who sees women as respectable upholders of the superego wants to outrage and defile the superego and the women who represent it.

There are many examples of husband defiance in the writings of Henry Miller, and as Kate Millett failed to recognise them, let us have a look at a quotation from *Sexus* in her book. As a friend of the family, Val is entitled to spend the night at the Woodruff house, followed by breakfast in bed while the husband goes off to work:

> "She hated the thought of waiting on men in bed. She didn't do it for her husband and she couldn't see why she should do it for me. To take breakfast in bed was something I never did except at Woodruff's place. I did it expressly to annoy and humiliate her."[2]

Kate Millett repeatedly draws attention to female rebellion against the sadistic domination by the male and his pleasure in squashing her rebellion. But she has no eye for the male rebellion against the moral norm. The earlier mentioned letter-writer (Ch.9) as well as Miller depict scenes of sexual defiance which are not merely

12. THE LIBERATION OF WOMEN

directed towards the woman but against the woman who is the property of another male; they degrade another man's property, they outrage the establishment male and they outrage the woman who is an establishment woman. One can say that they outrage the male superego in the woman, her defences against the libido, her refusal to have pleasure and to give pleasure.

Where dignity symbolises the authority of the superego it has to be attacked by degrading and defiling it. The woman who denies herself to the man in the name of purity and respectability will arouse his desire to defile her as an act of revenge. What the romantics and the pornographers of journalism and literature do is to remove the secondary repressions of perverse impulses. They uncover a mess, so to speak, that hides in the pre-conscious mind of inhibited men and women and the more 'liberated' they are the more freely they can expose it.

Let us be clear that the mess is not confined to the male. Female sadism is one of the deviations we found depicted in some of the more progressive journals of pornography as well as in the fantasies of the romantics. It is, however, still more repressed than male sadism as it meets more powerful cultural taboos, but in psychoanalytical practice one encounters it with considerable frequency. All of us are in the same boat here – both sexes victims of the superego which has for millennia denied us the right to express sexual pleasure freely.

If a woman liberationist considers man to be her enemy then she will consider sex to be the enemy; she will contribute to the negation of feminine pleasure. Women writers who see male sexuality as phallic, who confuse healthy genital sexuality with immature aggressive phallic sexuality will proclaim the sex act as an insult to women, as an act of degradation, as a humiliating experience. If the sex act is a humiliating experience, if to be penetrated means to be degraded then there is something fundamentally wrong with sex itself. Then they see sex as a means to perpetuate male dominance over women and the problem is reduced to sexism. Shulamith Firestone in her book *The Dialectic of Sex* does not hesitate to put the problem and its solution in the following way:

" ... the end goal of feminist revolution must be, unlike that of the first feminist movement, not just the elimination of male privilege but of the sex distinction itself: genital differences between human beings would no longer matter culturally. (A reversion to an unobstructed pansexuality, Freud's 'polymorphous perversity', would probably supersede hetero / homo / bi-sexuality.) The reproduction of the species by one sex for the benefit of both would be replaced by (at least the option of) artificial reproduction: children would be born to both sexes equally, or independently of either, however one chooses to look at it; the dependence of the child on the mother (and vice versa) would give way to a greatly shortened dependence on a small group of others in general, and any remaining inferiority to adults in physical strength would be compensated for culturally. The division of labour would be ended by the elimination of labour altogether (through cybernetics). The tyranny of the biological family would be broken."

Here we find it argued that the real source of the oppression of women by men lies in sex itself and the only way to overcome this biological injustice is the abolition of sexual differences.

I do not wish to discuss the nonsensicality of her statement but would draw attention to the anti-sexual attitude that emerges if men as such are seen as the enemies of women. If the receiving and yielding of a woman in the act of sex is seen as humiliation, if the woman's pleasure in natural sexuality is condemned, then femininity as such is condemned. Far from liberating woman and her sexual pleasure, a new type of puritanism is created. In the guise of anti-domination we find an anti-feminism, a denial of female sexuality, and we are back where we started – among the worst inanities of our puritan grandmothers. Under the guise of radicalism Shulamith Firestone projects a technological nightmare where most human functions would be performed by machines – including childbirth. In her 'utopia' she regards the abolition of differences between the sexes as the most important item:

12. THE LIBERATION OF WOMEN

"The freeing of women from the tyranny of reproduction by every means possible, and the diffusion of child-rearing to the society as a whole, to men and other children as well as women. This has been corrected. Child-bearing could be taken over by technology, and if this proved too much against our past tradition and psychic structure (as it certainly would at first) then adequate incentives and compensations would have to be developed – other than the ego rewards of possessing the child – to reward women for their special social contribution of pregnancy and childbirth."

In her mind equality between the sexes is achieved by sameness – she does not understand the difference between equality and sameness. In order to free women from humiliation we must, according to Miss Firestone, abolish femininity and overcome the natural biological functions. The important thing one must bear in mind here is that male castration fantasies lead to feminine self-castration fantasies. While Miss Firestone is somewhat extreme in her views, she is not alone in expressing them.

The aggression towards the male implies hostility against the male function in sex. If the male function in sex is seen as inevitably aggressive and nasty then the object of his desire – the female vagina, the soft radiance of her skin, the inviting lips, the excited eyes that beckon desire, the hair that flows as an intimation of female pride – then all these primary and secondary feminine characteristics are negated by the woman. The major victim in this negation process is the vagina. The joy of being penetrated is transformed into a sense of humiliation and the vagina will become anxious, defensive and self-negating. The sensations and pulsations in it, the rhythmic spasms manifesting a yearning for the male will be a source of fear and outrage in the woman who hates the male; she will stiffen her pelvis and her back, her legs will deny the vaginal sensations and will block the flow of the libido, they will refuse to be symbols of feminine eroticism; they will tighten, stiffen, they will either be held back in a rheumatic stubbornness or they will bang the ground in an assertion of independence. An armour of immobility and insensitivity will descend upon the erotogenic zones and her consciousness will arrive at the conclusion that there is no feeling in the vagina – in that place in which man would desire to dominate and degrade her. But in refusing the man entry, the woman often kills her libido and an emptiness of feeling will spread over her whole body which can only be counteracted by tensions. Then the pelvis and vagina tighten up, grip where there is nothing, and this creates an over-emphasis upon the clitoris, her own penis. If the woman cannot receive the penis then she will want to have one herself.

In varying degrees this process occurs in all girls from early childhood when the vagina, that sexual mouth that craves for nourishment and recognition, is frustrated and ignored. It happens to all those women who are repeatedly frustrated genitally and what woman in our culture, what child-woman is not frustrated and unacknowledged in her sexuality? Freud's definition of vaginal sexuality as a primacy which follows the clitoral primacy of girls has been revised by Karl Abraham and Melanie Klein, and traced back to early childhood. I have found evidence of vaginal sexuality during the first and second years. Particularly at the age of two, when the girl instinctively turns sexually towards father and has her first impulses to incorporate his penis orally and vaginally, the first traumas of rejection and denial usually appear. Girls' frequent fantasies of being raped by their fathers or brothers at that time, with particular emphasis upon oral rape, are usually the projection of their own desires. However, while these early sexual impulses and fantasies of the little girl are normally frustrated, a sense of being acknowledged by father and the communication of his libido and warmth to her will compensate to a great extent for the inevitable disappointment to infantile vaginal sexuality. If, however, the father fails to acknowledge the little girl as a girl-woman because of his own inhibitions then her feminine self-image will be stunted, she will feel rejected and unconfirmed in her identity and will develop a hostility to father that can have powerful repercussions upon her personality.

The vaginal libido is usually repressed after the second year owing to Oedipal guilt feelings and an early short-lived latency period follows. During that time she turns again towards mother

12. THE LIBERATION OF WOMEN

and identifies with her till at the age of about five a new vaginal sexuality and a renewed cathexis upon father appears. In the latency period the clitoral sensations increase to give way again to vaginal primacies during the age of about five and again at about thirteen. These developments are not merely biologically determined in a rigid manner but are greatly influenced by psychological factors, i.e. the parents' attitudes and the experiences and responses of the child. The development transformations can be distorted, that is to say the vaginal primacies may be disturbed and weakened and dominated by clitoral primacies.

The strength of the vaginal primacies depends upon the sexual responses and acknowledgement received from the males in the family, and by this I do not mean intercourse or overt sexual play – although this is desired by the child – but by unconscious body language, bodily responses like cuddling, playing, attention giving, etc. If these attentions from the father and the males in the family should fail to occur, the vaginal libido will be deprived and frustrated and the girl develops hostile and aggressive attitudes to the male and a variety of sadistic fantasies. Then clitoral sensations not only assume an important compensatory role but will continue to dominate right through the puberties of five and thirteen. Male identification on the part of the girl will in some degree establish itself and the males will appear as rivals. This type of rivalry with males can be quite normal and healthy in the latency periods when tomboyish attitudes often predominate to give way to the renewed feminine images at puberty. Should the male identification and the clitoral primacy persist, however, and fail to be replaced by the vaginal primacy, then the girl will inevitably feel the boy's penis to be infinitely more attractive than her tiny and often invisible clitoris and penis envy will emerge and become an important characteristic. It is thus the continued primacy of clitoral sexuality and the failure to arrive at a satisfactory vaginal image that is the chief cause for penis envy.

The aetiology of this curious manifestation in the sexual psychology of the female is more complex than it appears in Freud's formulations. Furthermore, it is not an instinctive or inevitable phenomenon but the result of the neglect of the vagina which girls so commonly experience in our culture. The predominance of clitoral sensations, the self-negation of the vaginal needs and the hostility to father often – but not always – create what we loosely call Lesbian predispositions. The essential factor here is that the vagina which does not receive love and acknowledgement from the primary males will hate the male who deprives her. As Reich put it: "If you don't love me I hate you." The girl who does not receive love as a female will hate not only the males but also her own feminine needs.

There are of course other important factors that contribute to Lesbianism and make it such a complex female syndrome. Father's hostility or indifference to mother, an overpowering and ruthless father or yet a too weak father, an inability or refusal to identify with mother, can in all various ways combine to create the complicated and varied characteristic we call Lesbianism. Lesbianism can of course be repressed and operate in a latent manner; a lack of female identification can produce a minor or major absence of vaginal genitality and a clitoral primacy among women who wish to relate to men but experience inadequacy feelings, sexual insecurity or a rivalry with men. On the other hand a powerful Oedipal rivalry with mother combined with a healthy vaginal primacy can lead a girl to rebel against the female superego norm which demands of her to be coy, restrained and passive in her behaviour. Perhaps we can call this type of reaction formation vaginal rebellion as against clitoral rebellion. These are just some of the possible combinations which emerge in the evolution of a female personality.

Many emancipated women seem to have a great need to prove that the clitoris is the real centre of female sexuality and that the vagina is relatively unimportant. If such women do not experience vaginal feelings because of neglect in childhood and have developed a dominant clitoral primacy, then they will need to make a virtue out of a weakness and generalise about the insensitivity of the vagina and the superiority of the clitoris. Also the negation of the vagina and emphasis upon the clitoris will reassure them in their desire not to be dependent upon men, and here again they will philosophise about feminine self-sufficiency in sex. Like other sexual deviationists they are great proselytisers.

12. THE LIBERATION OF WOMEN

VAGINAL VERSUS CLITORAL SEXUALITY

The researches of Masters and Johnson as well as Kinsey provide much ammunition for some of the chief propagandists of female liberation. Even the mechanistic and impersonal milieu of their observations seems to provide a welcome element to women who wish to escape the personal involvement and mutual dependencies that occur in genuine sexual relationships. It is true, as Germaine Greer points out, that "many women greeted the conclusions of Masters and Johnson with cries of – I told you so! I'm normal." And she continues:

> "If women find that the clitoris has become the only site of their pleasure instead of acting as a kind of sexual overdrive in a more general response, they will find themselves dominated by the performance ethic, which would not itself be a regression, if the performance principle in our society included enterprise and creativity. But enterprise and creativity are connected with libido which does not survive the civilising process." [3]

Referring to the permissive society with its mechanistic image of sexuality she says: "Sex for many has become a sorry business, a mechanical release, involving neither discovery nor triumph, stressing human isolation more dishearteningly than ever before." This is a refreshing voice expressing that aspect of female liberation which upholds the pride in feminine pleasure against the conventions of shame and repression. On the other side we see the vociferous propagandists of clitoral primacy. As their attention is fixed upon their phallic-clitoral primacy they are unduly preoccupied with the phallic characteristics of the male and have little difficulty in finding examples of it in literature as well as in reality. Their preoccupation with this characteristic in males evokes a castration anxiety in them, an image of the male as a castrator of women. Having themselves developed a phallic genitality which denies the receptivity and activity of the vagina, they see men as sexual aggressors and rapists. They do not, however, realise that the only relationship they are capable of with men is of a sado-masochistic type.

The phallic clitoris which stands in the way of vaginal gratification evokes paranoic fantasies of being violated and degraded; they project their masochistic urges upon men and then depict them as sadists. They unconsciously need sadistic men to liberate them from the phallic armour and their imagination is populated by male brutes and attackers and their writings will be redolent with protests against female degradation by men who are preoccupied with nothing else than crafty politics directed to the subjugation and rape of women. Politics will be seen as sex politics, as a male plot to oppress and defile women.

Another aspect of the phallic-clitoral predisposition of some women is their desire to establish the superiority of clitoral sexuality. This leads not only to 'scientific' theories intended to prove the sexual superiority of women but also to a mechanistic type of thinking. A typical example of this type of theoretising is Mary Jane Sherfey's book *The Nature and Evolution of Female Sexuality*, which has gained considerable importance in the female liberation movement. Dr. Sherfey is a New York psychiatrist and this book is mainly the reprint of a long article which appeared in 1966 in the journal of the Psychoanalytical Association. The main argument of the book is concerned with showing that the early embryo of human beings is female; secondly, that by the nature of their physiological structure women are sexually insatiable, and that civilisation arose as a means of suppressing the inordinate demands of female sexuality. She sets out to prove that the clitoris is not merely a residual organ of the penis and argues that the embryo is not undifferentiated sexually, as Freud assumed, but that it *is* a female. She bases this argument upon the assertion that without a great deal of androgen after the first five or six weeks no embryo would become a male, and therefrom concludes that the early embryos of human beings are female and would continue to be female if the androgen bath did not deflect some of them into becoming males. This argument has repeatedly been attacked and shown to be quite misleading because genetic or chromosomal sex is determined at the moment of fertilisation and it is quite incorrect to assume that the males are in any sense female prior to the androgen bath. Dr. Sherfey, however, takes the "innate femaleness of the mammalian embryos" as the rea-

12. THE LIBERATION OF WOMEN

son for thinking that the penis is an exaggerated clitoris and that the original libido is always feminine. She calls this the 'Adam out of Eve' myth which is a reversal of the 'Eve out of Adam' myth which she ascribes to Freud.

Her second thesis is based upon her interpretation of the work of Masters and Johnson. She describes the effect a paper of theirs had on her: "It was truly an eureka experience for me. This was it. Freud was wrong. Men are wrong, commonsense was wrong." Masters and Johnson have found that many females, especially when clitorally stimulated, can regularly have five or six orgasms within a matter of minutes. "Multiple orgasms are more apt to occur in auto-stimulation than with vaginal coition." They found that if the clitoris is given mechanical stimulation, as for instance, with an electric vibrator, some women could at times have twenty or more orgasms stopping only when they were totally exhausted. From this, some writers, including Dr. Sherfey, arrived at the conclusion that the clitoris is the real centre of feminine sexuality and that all women are inherently and basically multi-orgasmic, that they are more sexually endowed than men because the limit put to their orgastic experience is provided by man's inability to maintain an erection long enough to produce multiple orgasms in their partners. Dr. Sherfey's criterion of healthy and uninhibited sexual fulfilment in the woman is the number of orgasms which a woman can attain. From this it must follow that the clitoris is the centre of sexual stimulation and that masturbation or machine-induced vibration is the most fulfilling form of sexuality.

Many female liberationists have taken up Kinsey's statement that the vagina has no feelings at all and that vaginal orgasm is a myth. One woman liberationist has declared that: "It's wonderful that women have discovered masturbation because it will enable us to keep apart from men as long as necessary. When you have work to do, you can't allow yourself to be diverted by sexual relationships. Masturbation is what male revolutionists have always used to relieve themselves." [4]

That masturbation, particularly with an electric vibrator, is proven to be a superior form of sexuality than relationships with men is no doubt very gratifying to those women who want to be independent from men and are intent upon proving the superiority of female sexuality. As the superior vibrator and the multiple orgasms which it induces plays a large role in the imagination of some revolutionary women, let us have a look at what this type of orgasm is all about.

We have spoken earlier of the full discharge of sexual tension, the gratification of the libido in orgasm as a criterion of health and happiness – in particular in the theories of Wilhelm Reich – and we must ask whether the women with their clitorally induced multiple orgasms are gratified. What does it mean that women are "by nature sexually insatiable", as Dr. Sherfey and others claim? Are women by nature neurasthenics or nymphomaniacs? Or is there a basic misunderstanding in the concept of gratification when one speaks of women who experience a great number of orgasms terminating only in physical exhaustion? Is this physical exhaustion equivalent to gratification?

Let us be clear. It is true that some women can have perhaps two or three orgasms in intercourse and experience great satisfaction in it. Other women will have perhaps one orgasm and feel gratification and fulfilment while others may feel tense and unfulfilled after a great number of orgasms. Let us repeat here what we have stressed earlier: orgasm is a total bodily response involving a great number of libidinous primacies, muscular contractions that involve the whole body and its sensations, and in a woman is always marked by vaginal contractions. It involves the gratification, conscious and unconscious, of sexual needs, orgasm and the complete discharge of tensions. As Reich has put it: "The orgastic excitation results in lively contractions of the whole body musculature, culminating in release of tension and motor discharge."[5] We know that in people with chronic tensions and anxiety, certain muscular tensions remain and are not discharged in orgasm.

We have seen that in the clitoral primacy a tensing up of the vagina usually takes place. Clitoral stimulation, while often creating strong sensations of excitement, does not involve the discharge and release of many areas of muscular tension, particularly of the abdomen and pelvis. We notice among women who are restricted to clitoral sensations and excitement, a persistence

12. THE LIBERATION OF WOMEN

of tensions of their abdominal wall as well as of the muscles of the spinal column and pelvis. Masters and Johnson reported that by self-stimulation of the clitoral area: "A woman may experience five to twenty recurrent orgasmic experiences with the sexual tension never allowed to drop below a plateau phase maintenance level until physical exhaustion terminates the session." Now if a woman's sexual tension never drops below the plateau level even while she has a great number of orgasms till she drops with physical exhaustion, then we must conclude that by definition she has never arrived at an orgasm at all. If orgasm is followed by the resolution or relaxation phase, then one cannot have had an orgasm if the tension never drops below the pre-orgastic tension phase. And this is precisely what does not happen in multiple clitoral orgasms. What in fact occurs is a great number of orgasmic spasms without orgastic discharge.

During or after the experience of orgasmic spasms in women many parts of the body will remain tense, the libido needs remain unfulfilled and only physical exhaustion will put a stop to the pursuit of gratification. Masters and Johnson have also observed that women who frequently attain multiple orgasms with the vibrator "stop only when totally exhausted. Such sessions occurring two or three times a week created passive congestion of the pelvis and work hypertrophy of the clitoral shaft." The stimulations and excitements which they receive are more or less confined to one area which serves as stimulant, but the rest of the body does not respond in orgastic contractions nor in the release of tension.

Dr. Sherfey's observation that every instance of female orgasm leads to a further vasocongestion in the pelvic area is quite correct if we understand that what she calls orgasm is merely an orgastic spasm. Every orgastic spasm leads to increased tension whereas orgasm in the proper sense leads to parasympathicotonic release and expansion. Orgasmic spasms as such often generate a sense of irritation and frustration, while orgasm is accompanied by deep pleasure, gratitude and relaxation.

The argument about clitoral versus vaginal orgasm is fundamentally nonsensical because the clitoris acts as a highly sensitive stimulant that creates vaginal contractions and urges to receive and 'swallow' the penis. Clitoral and vaginal sensations act together to create that sense of fulfilment that comes from embracing and incorporating the penis in rhythmic movements which are similar to the infantile sucking reflex. This polemic is not directed against clitoral excitement but against clitoral exclusiveness which negates the vagina and the wholeness of female sexuality. It is important to observe that over-emphasis of the clitoris denies a woman many dimensions of the libido and causes her to be sexually one-dimensional. She represses many feelings of yearning, of receiving and giving which are central to a living being. Her musculature will usually remain tense and she will feel alienated from herself, experiencing sexual sensations in a mechanical fashion. Her predilection for mechanistic types of gratification shows a close inter-relation between erotic self-estrangement and mechanistic thinking. The mechanistically orientated person suffers from a lack of contact with self-feelings, from distrust of deep libidinous needs, from an armoured musculature. Sex mechanics and human engineering go close together and the sexual liberation movement that gets caught in mechanistic models of behaviour re-creates alienation and the barriers to freedom.

FREUD – THE CASTRATOR OF WOMEN

Another misrepresentation has gained much publicity and partial acceptance through the writings of some female liberationists, namely the accusation that Freud castrated women through his penis envy theory. Kate Millett, who was amongst the first to lead the attack upon Freud's "masculine sexual politics", calls him "beyond question the strongest counter-revolutionary force in the ideology of sexual politics." She writes:

> "Beginning with the theory of penis envy, the definition of the female is negative – what she is is the result of the fact that she is not a male and 'lacks' a penis. Freud assumed that the female's discovery of her sex is, in and of itself, a catastrophe of such vast proportions that it haunts a woman

12. THE LIBERATION OF WOMEN

all through life and accounts for most aspects of her temperament. His entire psychology of women, from which all modern psychology and psychoanalysis derives heavily, is built upon an original tragic experience – born female."

She asks some pertinent questions, but accuses Freud of patriarchal bias by pointing to his concern with the observation of drives and fantasies and apparently ignoring social influences:

"Either maleness is indeed an inherently superior phenomenon, and in which case its 'betterness' could be empirically proved and demonstrated, or the female misapprehends and reasons erroneously that she is inferior. And again, one must ask why. What forces in her experience, her society and socialisation have led her to see herself as an inferior being? The answer would seem to lie in the conditions of patriarchal society and the inferior position of women within this society. But Freud did not choose to pursue such a line of reasoning, preferring instead an aetiology of childhood experience based upon the biological fact of anatomical differences."

Freud's discovery that the female castration complex exists was of fundamental importance and an important corollary to the male castration complex. Before one can ask why these phenomena existed, one must first discover them and observe how they developed in the individual. The accusation against Freud of bias is particularly nonsensical, as it is directed against a man who, with unbelievable courage, followed his observations into directions which were unacceptable to most people and who, without compunction, entered into the most closely guarded secrets of the human mind. Observe how carefully Freud goes about defining the differences between men and women and how with his emphasis upon bi-sexuality he broke through many long-established barriers between the sexes:

"We speak of a human being, whether male or female, behaving in a masculine or feminine way. But you will at once observe that that is simply following the lead of anatomy and convention. You can give the concepts of masculine and feminine *no* new content. The difference is not a psychological one; when you say 'masculine' you mean as a rule 'active', and when you say 'feminine' you mean 'passive'. Now it is quite true that there is such a correlation. The male sexual cell is active and mobile; it seeks out the female one, while the latter, the ovum, is stationary, and waits passively. This behaviour of the elementary organisms of sex is more or less a model of the behaviour of the individuals of each sex in sexual intercourse. The male pursues the female for the purpose of sexual union, seizes her and pushes his way into her. But with that you have, so far as psychology goes, reduced the quality of masculinity to the factor of aggressiveness. You will begin to doubt whether you have hit upon anything fundamental here, when you consider that in many classes of animals the female is the stronger and more aggressive party, and the male is only active in the single act of sexual intercourse. That is the case, for instance, with spiders. The functions of caring for the young, too, and of rearing them, which seem to us so essentially feminine, are not, among animals, always associated with the female sex. In some species of animals, quite high in the scale, one finds that the sexes share in the duties of looking after the young, or even that the male devotes himself to it alone. Even in the sphere of human sexual life, one soon notices how unsatisfactory it is to identify masculine behaviour with activity and feminine with passivity. But I advise you not to do that. It seems to me to serve no good purpose and to give us no new information.

 Both sexes seem to pass through the early phases of libidinal development in the same way. One might have expected that already in the sadistic-anal phase we should find that the girl showed less aggressiveness; but this is not the case. Women analysts have found from the analysis of children's play that the aggressive impulses of little girls leave nothing to be desired as regards copiousness and violence." [5]

12. THE LIBERATION OF WOMEN

He proved that penis envy does occur in little girls, not only from the psychoanalysis of adults but from the observations and analysis of children carried out by such female analysts as Dr. Ruth Mack Brunswick, Dr. Jean Lampl de Groot, Dr. Helene Deutsch, Anna Freud, Melanie Klein, and many others. Furthermore, any observant mother will notice occasional or even persistent manifestations of penis envy in girls "who also want to have it."

Once the infantile development of the girl has been studied, one can ask why the girl feels a sense of deprivation in not having a penis. I have asked these questions and give a short explanation of them in the passages dealing with vaginal repression and the clitoral primacies. I have no doubt that vaginal repressions are due to the sex-restricting taboos of patriarchy which are responsible not only for penis envy but a great many other complexes in both men and women.

But let us not blame Freud for having discovered penis envy. He had many accusations thrown at him for his discoveries which upset men's narcissism and challenged their repressions. His injury to the female narcissism is but one of many such injuries. The courage to observe unconscious processes and to acknowledge them necessarily precedes attempts to rectify them. In all his writings on female penis envy Freud was careful not to commit himself to an explanation based on biological necessity. Like Reich, Malinowski and others, I do not believe that the Oedipus complex or female penis envy is universal or inevitable. They are both aspects of sexual repression which is prevalent in patriarchy.

THE SEXUAL CLASS WAR

Many women find a theoretical basis for female liberation in the Marxian concept of dialectical materialism which, in the words of Engels, "is the view of history that seeks the ultimate cause and the great moving power of all historical events in the economic development of society." More and more women accept the notion that if you are oppressed in society it must be for economic reasons and that women must recognise that they belong to an exploited class. While men are exploited as industrial wage slaves, so women are exploited as wives, and the overthrow of the family is as important as the overthrow of the capitalist system. They maintain that because women are not paid wages for their housework they are exploited not merely by the bourgeois system but also by their husbands, and insist that women can only be free if they become fully-fledged members of the productive system with equal pay, equal opportunities and equal skills.

We have seen a proliferation of oppressed classes, i.e. the youth class, the student class, the class of the sexually repressed and now the exploited class of women, all taking their place beside the working class whose class-consciousness has diminished in the consumer society and needs to be strengthened by new arrivals. By refusing to allow themselves to be oppressed any longer by the family structure, women would strike a blow at the foundations of capitalism and authoritarianism. Germaine Greer who, unlike some of her comrades, avoids heavy demagogy, puts her suggestions for the tactics and aims of the female revolution in her typically charming and expressive manner:

> "The key to the strategy of liberation lies in exposing the situation and the simplest way to do it is to outrage the pundits and the experts by sheer impudence of speech and gesture, the exploitation of cliché 'feminine logic' to expose masculine pomposity, absurdity and injustice. Women's weapons are traditionally their tongues, and the principal revolutionary tactic has always been the spread of information. Now as before, women must refuse to be meek and guileful, for truth cannot be served by dissimulation. Women who fancy that they manipulate the world by pussy power and gentle cajolery are fools."

Her revolutionary aim she puts as follows:

> "Only by experimentation can we open up new possibilities which will indicate lines of development in which the *status quo* is a given term. Women's revolution is necessarily situationist: we cannot argue that all will be well when the socialists have succeeded in abolishing private property and

12. THE LIBERATION OF WOMEN

restoring public ownership of the means of production. We cannot wait that long. Women's liberation, if it abolishes the patriarchal family, will abolish a necessary substructure of the authoritarian state, and once that withers away Marx will have come true willy-nilly, so let's get on with it." [6]

The notion that women can establish a better society *against men*, that as a class of their own they can fight all other classes which are subsumed under the title 'the male class', as well as against the reactionary members of their own class, is too absurd to merit serious consideration. It completely perverts and caricatures Marxism or any possible variant of it, and merely shows the desperation of progressive minds in Western society, their atomisation and their alienation from the realities of life.

Women can and ought to be in the vanguard of radicalism and social change, but they must, like their male colleagues, understand the instruments of repression and oppression that operate in patriarchy. They might be a leading force in a real struggle for human liberation from an authoritarian psyche and an authoritarian system; they might lead in the fight against an authoritarian repressive superego whose victims they have been for so long. The relationship between men and women is determined by the norms which consciously and unconsciously determine our behaviour to each other and to ourselves, and if men have repressed women it is because they have been repressed themselves.

If women want to fight the establishment by fighting against men then they merely reinforce the stultification of the libido, the love between the sexes which according to Marx "is life, all that is immediate, all sensuous experience, all real experience." Marx believed that "the immediate, natural necessary relation of human being to human being is the relation of man to woman ... the relation of man to woman is the most natural relation of human being to human being."

The most powerful force in the struggle against a life-denying establishment is Eros, while anything that undermines it only upholds and strengthens the Thanatos-ridden superego. There are no free men *or* free women – there are only free human beings. Human freedom is not divisible into sexes.

1. John Milton: *Paradise Lost*.
2. Kate Millett: *Sexual Politics* (Abacus, 1972).
3. Germaine Greer: *The Female Eunuch* (Paladin, 1971).
4. Quoted in 'The Liberated Orgasm' by Barbara Seaman.
5. Sigmund Freud: Lecture 33 'Femininity', *New Introductory Lectures on Psychoanalysis*.
6. Germaine Greer: *The Female Eunuch* (Paladin, 1971).

13. An Epidemic of Male Impotence

How do men react to the sexually liberated woman? Many find her fascinating and stimulating, in contrast to the traditionally coy and reserved woman who has caused men a great deal of frustration and trouble. That women nowadays are able to affirm their own sexual needs is certainly encouraging for a man and releases him, in a large measure, from feelings of guilt.

But let us remember that neither the modern woman nor modern man has much capacity for uninhibited sexuality and warmth. All too often we find instead a clash between female assertiveness and traditional male dominance – a clash between the sexual aggression of the male and the female. Superficially women seem to be winning the battle as the progressive male tends to sympathise with women's struggle for equality and dignity and takes her side against the tradition of male domination.

But a growing number of doctors, psychiatrists and social workers are reporting a new sexual crisis which they claim is beginning to assume epidemic proportions. Some call it the "new impotence", others "the crisis of masculinity". It is alleged that this crisis is the focus of the greatest sexual debate in America since the Kinsey Report. Some of these reports tend to be rather sensational and have been ridiculed by female liberationists. There is, however, a genuine problem here, and it is my opinion that male impotence, particularly among the young, is on the increase.

We can observe three aspects of the "new impotence":
1. The inhibited rage of the dominant male against the aggressive or liberated woman.
2. Unisex patterns and incest taboo.
3. The submissive male who welcomes the dominant woman as a mother-figure.

1. In the sexuality of the traditional male, aggression plays an important part. His sexuality was associated with economic power and dominance over the dependent woman. He assumed responsibility for the 'natural law of procreation' and saw to it that women accepted their duties as wives and mothers. While the woman was seen to be passive by nature, men were the agents of reproduction as well as of wealth and social progress. Men had to impose their will upon life, upon society and women, and be ready to fight at all times. So it is no wonder that their sexuality absorbed a considerable quantum of aggressive and sadistic libido, and the penis became a weapon, a symbol of power and aggression which we call phallic. A man's power and the woman's admiration and gratitude were important aspects of sexual desirability and sexual arousal. The yielding, responsive, appreciative woman was sexually stimulating and desirable while the new woman, who does not need to be conquered, who does not need to submit to male sexuality but demands it as a right and does not become dependent upon the male, undermines his patterns of sexual desire. She will appear to him as a strange creature, as a non-woman, even as a rival or disguised male. The woman's demand for equality is either resented by the dominant male or it will appear as a threat to his superiority and unconsciously arouse castration anxieties.

If such a man happens to be progressive and intellectual, he will support the woman's claims for equality, repress his sexual aggression, accept her as the ideal type of woman, seek her out and often find himself impotent with her. On the other hand the men of the assertive phallic type who are not intellectual or particularly concerned with advanced or progressive ideas concerning women will treat these modern women as 'women'. They 'know how to treat women' and have not been confused by the new morality; they will either ignore women's claims of equality or reject them as undesirable. The interesting thing is that an increasing number of progressive women find the type of man who typifies uninhibited male aggressiveness, very attractive and the only ones able to satisfy them sexually. Reports abound of educated upper-class women frequenting working men's clubs and pubs to pick up men for sexual satisfaction. These women use

13. AN EPIDEMIC OF MALE IMPOTENCE

such men sexually to satisfy their deep-seated masochism, at the same time revenging themselves upon them by being conscious of their own social and intellectual superiority. They do not need to compete with these men and are therefore able to vent their masochistic urges which they could not do with their social equals without losing face. With men of their own class these women have to compete in order to assert their equality. Their preference for the lower class male is an insult to men in general, for it implies that the man who is socially successful and is respected as a person, is sexually inadequate, while the man who is sexually adequate is inferior as a person. Girls who were treated as inferiors by father, brothers and other boys now find revenge in sexual superiority over the males of their own class and personal superiority over men of a lower class.

The 'gamekeeper' syndrome has been the subject of a considerable amount of psychoanalytical study. But what used to be regarded as a neurosis is now seen as a norm. While the non-intellectual man dismisses these women or ignores their claims for equality, the intellectual feels he has to sympathise with them. The interesting thing is that it is precisely the sympathetic progressive male who, repressing his instinctive aggression, is likely to become impotent, while the reactionary male, who couldn't care less, will retain his virility.

2. One of the ways in which sexual equality manifests itself in young people is in the cult of unisex. Unisex abolishes sexual differences, emphasising similarities between the sexes rather than differences. When the 'specific functions of the female' (like looking after children and the home) are seen as inferior activities limiting a woman's personality, and male activities (such as working in factories, sweeping the streets, emptying dustbins, building and making things, running business and enterprises of all kinds) are considered as being expressive of the higher human faculties, then equality for women means participation in these activities.

Typical female occupations are considered to be a stigma of enslavement and inferiority and any self-respecting woman should resent being bound to them. Insofar, however, as many of these 'feminine' activities are essential for the purposes of living, equality between the sexes means equal participation in them. Any man in the least concerned with sexual equality would be expected to cook, wash up, knit, sew, change nappies, clean the home, take the children to school and look after their clothes: he is expected to join in these activities together with the woman. Work is to be interchangeable between the sexes and all taboos relating to the difference between the work of a man or woman should be abolished.

It is also argued that children should no longer be trained or conditioned into acquiring a specifically male or female self-image. Boys should be given dolls to play with, taught to sew, cook and to baby-mind; girls should be encouraged to use tools, play with trains, bows and arrows and all other toys usually reserved for boys and considered masculine. Women liberationists claim that the traditional male and female image is inculcated in children by the toys they are given and the games they are encouraged to play. They particularly challenge the Freudian assumptions that boys are inherently aggressive and that the genital characteristics of the male predispose him to play-activities which symbolise the aggressive penetrative urges of his sex. The sports which are a collective symbolisation of male virility and aggressive power are, according to female liberationists, no more than the encouragement of male aggression, determination and power from which women were deliberately debarred in the past.

It could be argued that all human activities should be engaged in equally by the sexes if we wish to affirm the right to full human self-expression for all. But the matter is not really as simple as that. It is true that one must have reservations about theories that uphold the biological and intrinsic differences between the sexes and their respective roles and activities in society. We know too much about the bi-sexuality of human beings, particularly the factor of cultural conditioning which creates sexual roles and identities. But having said this, we must consider that there are cultural differences between male and female orientated thinking.

13. AN EPIDEMIC OF MALE IMPOTENCE

A patriarchal culture has a framework of goals and assumptions, patterns of thinking, which are different from those of a matriarchal culture. For instance, the cultivation of abstract thought as manifested in logic, law and science, the hierarchic concept of society and of nature, contrasts with the personal, subjective and intuitive type of thinking which one would find dominant in a matriarchal culture. (I am emboldened to make this generalisation in view of the evidence unearthed by archaeologists in recent years concerning the arts and symbols of matriarchal cultures dating back some 10,000 to 20,000 years, as well as by the examples of recent matriarchal cultures investigated by Margaret Mead, Malinowski and others.) Their art, fantasies and imagination would be of a different kind and create different spiritual superstructures.

We face the fact that our culture and its complex artefacts of religions, laws, science, technology, business and the hierarchical orientations represent the dominant male superego. I am not introducing here a value judgment, for I am fully aware that patriarchal compulsions and symbolisations have created much suffering and that humanity has to overthrow many of them in order to survive. *Here* I am concerned with the effect which the undermining of this culture and the subsequent blurring of roles between the sexes is having upon the sexuality of the male.

In our culture male sexuality is associated with discovery and conquest and especially with exogamy – where the boy has to turn away from the familiar women of his tribe and seek the strange and unknown woman in the world outside. The Oedipus complex and incest taboo compel him to desexualise the familiar woman and direct his sexuality to women outside his home or family. We know that over-familiarity with girls will dull the sexual interest of the boy towards them and he will, apparently inexplicably, go searching for girls on the other side of the hill. The desexualisation of the familiar woman and the sexualisation of the unknown and unfamiliar is not merely a peculiar trick of patriarchal fantasy – it is the very basis of cultural diffusion and expansion.

Germaine Greer writes:

"When Adam saw Eve in the Garden of Eden he loved her because she was of himself, bone of his bone, and more like him than any of the other animals created for his delectation. His movement of desire towards her was an act of love for his own kind. This kind of diffuse narcissism has always been accepted as a basis for love, except in the male–female relationship where it has been assumed that man is inflamed by what is different in women, and therefore the differences have been magnified until men have more in common with other men of different races, creeds and colours than they have with the women of their own environment."

She forgets, however, to mention that Adam and Eve were made to wear fig leaves once they discovered sexual love. In fact she has got it all wrong. Adam and Eve lived as brother and sister before they ate from the Tree of Knowledge and discovered the differences between them. It was only then that they fell in love sexually and had to hide their genitals behind the fig leaf. It was the fig leaf which symbolised their sexuality, and it was not long before they had to leave Paradise – the infantile world of security where sexual love was forbidden. They had to go out into the strange world where they had to work for a living and could enjoy sex.

The female liberationists want us to drop our fig leaves, so that we can look at each other and recognise our humanity in each other and consider ourselves members of one big family. But the old Adam has his doubts and he sees behind the voice of the female a defiance of God and an incestuous seduction. If we become members of one big family sharing the same interests and pursuing the same activities we might learn to love one another, but the incestuous fears and the wrath of God with his Oedipus complex will desexualise our relationships. As Germaine Greer has rightly observed: "If Denis Law hugs Nobby Stiles on the football pitch we tolerate it because it is not love" – or we might say we tolerate it because in the love between the two there is no sexual element. There is evidence that the sexual tension and excitement between the sexes is lost in the unisex familiarity. We can observe in many long-lasting marriage relationships

13. AN EPIDEMIC OF MALE IMPOTENCE

a certain incestuous quality while the 'other woman', the unknown mysterious temptress and adventuress hovers threateningly over the marital horizon.

Woman wants to emerge from the stigma of being different which has set a strict barrier to her activities; she is tired of being a mystery and, as such, shut off from the 'real' activities of the world; she wants to leave the confines of the family and become a mate, a sister, a fellow-worker. But the danger is that she may experience the same fate as Nobby Stiles on the football pitch. More and more unisex couples find that something is missing. They experience boredom and inexplicable anxiety as, without realising it, they repress their sexuality in their love for each other.

Furthermore, it is interesting to notice a latent hostility which emerges in unisex relationships, particularly on the part of the male. Behind the postures of loving sameness I have frequently noticed extraordinary outbursts of viciousness which cause distress and puzzlement to both partners. The boredom of unisex is indeed already emerging as a problem despite the ideological satisfactions of this new way of loving. If one looks closely at people who advocate this type of relationship then one notices an urge to identify with the other sex, an attraction of sameness which is due to a desire for identification rather than an object relationship. Let me explain the difference. In identification we introject the object into ourselves, we experience the other in ourselves and love it by being like him or her. Imitation is an important aspect of love by identification. We recognise the other in ourselves or conversely recognise ourselves in the other and by falling in love we experience a narcissistic gratification. This also leads to the satisfactions of vicarious living through the other person's experiences as if they were our own. Although there is always a measure of narcissism in a loving relationship, we do not really love the other person for his own sake if narcissism predominates, but we merely love ourself in him or her. An object relationship expresses the capacity of an *I–Thou* relationship where we experience the other person's feelings and his mind and are capable of empathising with him. We love him because of what he makes us feel; we love him as a new discovery that adds a new dimension to ourselves. In identification, on the other hand, we love others because they are like ourselves; we move in a closed circuit of self-love that desires sameness and tolerates no new additions to self-experience.

Unisex not only undermines the attractions of polarity but also revives incest taboos which dominate the relationship of brothers and sisters. It is not so much the case that there is no sexual attraction between children – psychoanalysis has found plenty of evidence for it – but that this attraction is repressed. In unisex the boy and girl unconsciously return to a brother and sister relationship and encounter the desexualising influences of incest taboos.

Unisex is also to some extent a denial of heterosexuality and a form of homosexuality. We have the man who wishes to experience feminine sensations through the woman and also the woman who wants to experience her masculine sensations and urges through the male. Sometimes we find that the latent homosexual element in unisex takes the form of a tacit agreement to engage in sexual relationships outside the 'marriage', and a vicarious participation in each other's excitement and adventures. We find this expressed in many novels as, for instance, in the classic *Les Liaisons Dangereuses*, where the two partners have an agreement to seduce as many people as possible and compare notes of their respective exploits. D. H. Lawrence's menage with Frieda von Richthofen was of a similar nature as they arranged their home as a kind of spider's web to entangle friends and visitors in a sexual trap.

Unisex is all right for couples who share a disposition to identify with the other sex or have homosexual propensities, but if it is propagated as a norm it can create considerable sexual disturbances and may lead to impotence.

3. The 'new female' sometimes attracts the submissive type of man who seeks a domineering woman as a mother surrogate. He will seek in her the love and protection of mother and desexualise both her and himself in an essentially incestuous relationship. Men with domineering, devouring mothers and a weak or much absent father will preconsciously yearn for a mother-figure in a

13. AN EPIDEMIC OF MALE IMPOTENCE

woman from whom they want protection and love. Sometimes they will strive to get satisfaction with women outside the incestuous bond and may become the Don Juan type, only to reject these women for the fantasy mother whom they fundamentally desire but with whom they are impotent.

Alexander Portnoy – that extraordinary creation of Philip Roth – had his mother so deeply ingrained in him that "for the first year in school I seem to have believed that each of my teachers was my mother in disguise." He tried to rid himself of her influence by a large number of perverse fantasies and acts with "outside" women, mostly Christian. While he abandons himself in these activities and often experiences intense excitement, there is always something else he wants and none of his sexual partners can satisfy him. When he goes to Israel, his spiritual and maternal home, he is impotent with both women he tries to have sex with. No doubt the Israeli women represent his protective all-loving mother whom he cannot get out of his mind but cannot allow himself to love sexually.

There has never been a shortage of domineering females who, to everybody's surprise, have found men to love them, but nowadays they struggle to be accepted as the prototype of the normal and healthy woman and attract mother-smothered males. Many men who would have previously repressed their submissive mother-dependent inclinations now openly seek out this type of woman and find they are impotent with them.

I must also mention that the task-performing element of sexuality referred to earlier, where the man has to prove himself adequate to the demands of the sexually knowledgeable woman, can undermine not only his confidence but also his spontaneity. Sex as a deliberate performance to satisfy the woman de-automatises the sexual reflexes and can disturb the involuntary processes of orgasm. Man's need to prove himself also creates anger and anxiety, as the woman will be seen as a judge instead of as a partner involved with him in mutual sexual desire. Rollo May has observed: "The emphasis beyond a certain point on technique in sex makes for a mechanistic attitude towards love-making and goes along with alienation, feelings of loneliness and depersonalisation."[1]

These are some of the deviations that are being encouraged by the sexual revolution, bringing with them "the puzzlement of the penis" as described in Dr. Spielvogel's (Portnoy's analyst) immortal thesis. The new sexual roles which men are supposed to play often arouse their unconscious resentment which expresses itself in impotence as a kind of revenge against the demands of women.

1. Rollo May: *Love and Will* (Fontana, 1972).

14. Conclusions and Beginnings

In his book *The Sexual Revolution* Reich describes the initial stage in the treatment of neurosis: "Character analytic treatment releases the vegetative energies from their fixations and their armour. The immediate result of this is an intensification of the antisocial and perverse impulses and with that of social anxiety." In my own work with patients I also find that the liberation of libido energy initially releases aggressive and sadistic urges previously not conscious to the patient. If we consider the sexual revolution as a mass therapy then we must realise that it has got stuck in the first stage. Let us see how Reich explains the next stage of therapy:

> "When one begins to dissolve the infantile fixations to the parental home, to the infantile traumata and the antisexual taboos, more and more energy finds its way to the genital system ... While previously the whole thinking and acting was determined by unconscious, irrational motives, the patient now becomes increasingly capable of acting and reacting rationally. In the course of this process, inclinations to mysticism, religiosity, infantile dependence, superstitious beliefs, etc., disappear more and more, without the exertion of any 'educational' influence on the patient. While previously the patient was completely armoured, incapable of contact with himself and his environment, capable only of unnatural pseudocontacts, he now develops an increasing capacity for immediate, natural contact with his impulses as well as his environment. The result of this is a visible

development of natural, spontaneous behaviour instead of the previous unnatural, artificial behaviour."

The capacity for full orgastic gratification and the abolition of orgasm anxiety, the capacity for immediate natural contact free from personal distrust and tribal paranoia and the development of natural spontaneous behaviour was still the aim of the sexual revolution seen as a mass therapy.

At the present time we are still very much in the first stage of the therapy and I am concerned to draw attention to this in order to prevent advocates of the sexual liberation from mistaking the phenomena of the initial stage for the cure. For if we forget the aims of the therapy, i.e. the aims of the sexual revolution, then the released aggressive and perverse drives will acquire dominance and parade as freedom.

It would be disturbing if, for instance, a depressive patient in the early part of treatment were to consider his released sadistic impulses as a norm of health to be emulated by others. It is equally disturbing if a society undergoing the experience of sexual liberation were to become fixated upon the first stage, content with the release of hostility and perversion and with a mechanistic attitude to sex, declaring it as the cure, as the achievement of freedom. This would be an arrest in the development of liberation, a diversion from the quest for the wholeness of sexual experience and of being, and would be a kind of decadence before the liberation even got under way. The toleration of such a state of affairs would undermine the potentials inherent in human freedom. While the pioneers of the sexual revolution intended to overcome the root causes of the authoritarian structure of individuals and of society, i.e. sexual repression – the sexual liberation movement of our time has only removed the secondary repressions and left the primary repressions intact.

So we see a multitude of perversions which previously were held in check bursting to the surface and masquerading as freedom. Having removed the inhibitions against them we can act them out more freely but we are no more in contact with our primary libido than before. We are still alienated from ourselves.

We can see a similar situation in the socio-political sphere.

14. CONCLUSIONS AND BEGINNINGS

With the breakdown of religious and state authority there occurs a release of pent-up aggression and violence. The superego no longer has the power to contain the anger against it by the traditional method of channelling it against other States or religions, partly because thermonuclear weapons have made major wars too risky.

There is no doubt that we are entering an era of civic violence and political guerrilla warfare, and most striking is the notion that violence against authority is in itself a realisation of freedom. In the past freedom was seen as an alternative social condition and the revolutionary struggle a means for its establishment: now the struggle itself is elevated into a realisation of freedom. The arguments about ends and means which were central to the writings of Orwell and Koestler are ignored and means have become ends. There is nothing beyond. It is all here and now. And here and now is violence, the activism of hate in which a man's identity as a free being is supposed to be realised. Fight against the oppressors and you are already free!

The analogy between the socio-political liberation of secondary drives and the sexual liberation of secondary drives is all too obvious. Those who are concerned with freedom as an alternative to repression and hatred should recognise the real aim of freedom – the fulfilment of man's primary urges, his freedom to love and to be acknowledged as a whole person – and see the present liberation in its proper perspective. Alienated people who have no awareness of the process of becoming and of development, who cannot comprehend the aim of freedom, will mistake the freedom of aggression for freedom itself. Thus they will not only cause much misery but make the achievement of freedom impossible. They end up as reactionaries who are content with hate; they do not understand that love, work and knowledge (as Reich put it) are the mainsprings of life. They are reactionaries shutting the door to freedom, finding satisfaction in fighting, inviting other reactionaries to fight them and we have a battlefield of perverse gratifications.

It is, as I have said, necessary to have a theoretical understanding of the stages of liberation from sexual repression and social oppression and to encourage an understanding of freedom both in sexuality as well as in the socio-political field. These two are of course inter-related. They are two dimensions of one reality. To comprehend what freedom is gives significance to the means by which it is to be achieved.

In the individual treatment of the neuroses it is left to the therapist to have an understanding of what health means and to make an effort to direct his patient's attention to it, to make him aware of the significance of released aggression in relation to the sexual needs still repressed. While of course it is wrong to impose rigid concepts, the art of the therapist lies in his ability to gauge the authentic needs of his patient's libido and open his eyes to them. Thus the treatment is necessarily patient-orientated, but it needs the help of the therapist to overcome the patient's alienation from himself. In the same way a definition of socio-political or sexual freedom must not be merely an effort to impose one's own idiosyncracies upon people and imagine that by doing so one liberates them. This has been the fate of many Utopias.

> "But what is historically possible cannot be achieved simply by a straightforward progression of the immediately given (with its 'laws'), but only by a consciousness of the whole of society acquired through manifold mediations, and by a clear aspiration to realise the dialectical tendencies of history. And the series of mediations may not conclude with unmediated contemplation: it must direct itself to the qualitatively new factors arising from the dialectical contradictions: it must be a movement of mediations advancing from the present to the future."[1]

The future becomes possible if the present is released from its anchorings in the past. The next stage, therefore, is to become conscious of our fixations upon infantile traumas and taboos and on the social level to become aware of our fixations upon mystical and irrational concepts which determine our society. If we can make our individual and social fixations conscious and if we can release our energies from their unconscious anchorings the ego may find a new way to satisfy our primary needs for love and acceptance; the capacity for choice can take over from

14. CONCLUSIONS AND BEGINNINGS

the reign of compulsion. While the determinants of our behaviour and our thoughts remain unconscious, we are obliged to act them out compulsively and defeat all efforts for individual and social sanity.

The central core and determinant of the taboos and inhibitions which dominate patriarchy is the Oedipus complex. From it stems pleasure anxiety, submissiveness to and glorification of authority, fear of intellectual and emotional spontaneity, mistrust of oneself and of others, social and individual paranoia, as well as the processes of splitting, projection, alienation and reification which we have discussed earlier. The Oedipus complex is anchored in the family and reproduces itself in society with its authoritarian symbols of power and its hierarchic order. The Oedipus complex causes us to be in awe of authority, compelling us to adopt submissive and sacrificial or aggressive attitudes which, as we have seen, have made freedom impossible both on the social and on the personal level. The most important project of the sexual and social revolution must therefore be the abolition of the Oedipus complex. As the Oedipus complex is the result of patriarchy and in turn perpetuates it, its abolition means the abolition of patriarchy. This must be the long-term aim of true radicalism.

Let us first understand the size of the task. Let us understand that the abolition of patriarchy means nothing less than the creation of a new culture. It is not concerned merely with changes in institutions, for we have seen that new institutions will quickly absorb the compulsions of patriarchy. Radicalism now must be concerned with a fundamental cultural transformation. We know that the foundations of a culture are created in the infantile experiences shared by its members, and that the repression of the libido creates symbols and complexes which become the dominant orientations in society. This knowledge might make us despair of ever breaking through the fundamental psychic structures that operate in a culture or to wait for future generations of better brought-up people to create a culture without guilt and paranoia. In the heyday of psychoanalytic hope there used to be a saying meant to be funny: if you really want to succeed in psychoanalysing a person, you have to start with his grandparents. We cannot wait that long, and in any case nothing ever happens by passively hoping for it.

I visualise two stages in the cultural transformation ahead of us. Firstly, we must create a milieu, an ideology if you like, where people learn that the capacity of experiencing sexual pleasure, not only genitally but in all the bodily functions, is a virtue to be encouraged; while the negation of pleasure experiences both in ourselves as well as in others, and the spreading of guilt, is evil. At the same time we must help parents to realise that the communication of libido pleasures to their children is essential for their development into healthy and free persons.

Secondly, we must subject the life-negating characteristics of our culture to a critical analysis, relating them to the compulsions of patriarchy, and then conceptualise a society which is free from patriarchal fixations and compulsions. If one learns to trace complex behaviour patterns in individuals to the Oedipus complex and the destructive compulsions of societies to patriarchy, then one paves the way for the psychological and cultural transformation which will be necessary in the not too distant future.

While it is inevitable that the small child sees its parents as huge and all-powerful beings who, as Freud pointed out, are later transformed into images of omnipotent deities, it is not necessary for these images to be frightening. It is the sexual conflicts of patriarchy which fundamentally transform the primal objects into symbols of anxiety and even terror, creating fixations and over-dependency and making the process of maturation and the achievement of freedom exceedingly difficult.

Let us look at some of the taboos which a child encounters in the family. This is not just a matter of inhibitions of sexual genitality, although these are of major importance. It firstly concerns the child's reactions towards its own polymorphous erotic sensations. We have mentioned that the mother who experiences pleasure at breast-feeding will communicate pleasure to the child's oral activities and furthermore a sense of pleasure in itself, a sense of being loved and wanted. But how can a mother communicate pleasure to the child if she herself is anxious, frustrated and inhibited? This does not only relate to breast-feeding, but also to her communication of peripheral pleasure by cuddling and

14. CONCLUSIONS AND BEGINNINGS

caressing and her attitudes to anal and urethral functions. If any of these processes arouse the mother's unconscious anxiety and evokes a forbidding or demanding attitude in her, then one can be quite sure that retentive, compulsive character attitudes or neuroses will appear in the child, influencing it as an adult and in turn reproducing similar reactions in her children.

One has to propagate the truth that breast-feeding, cuddling, caressing, urination, defaecation, eating and drinking are not merely physical activities to be pursued mechanically in the right quantities and at the right times but are sources of pleasure: that the libido component of all these functions is just as important, if not more so than their physical aspects. If we want a child to breast-feed correctly then the mother must allow herself the erotic sensations which arise during the sucking. It is worthwhile mentioning in this connection that sucking creates vaginal sensations in women which in turn arouses unconscious inhibitions of the libido component of suckling. One must be able to enjoy the pleasures of one's own biological activities and not dissociate oneself from one's own body as if it were an alien thing. If you can have pleasure in your natural activities then you can communicate them to the child and, all being well, the child will learn to consider itself as a source of pleasure – it will consider itself good, clean, beautiful and friendly. The difficulty is to avoid compulsive attitudes which so many progressives adopt in these matters when they want to do the right thing by their child while at the same time suffering agonies of guilt and insecurity.

Let us reiterate that self-experience of pleasure is the correct foundation for the communication of pleasure. The important thing is that with the sensation of pleasure in the natural functions these would cease to be considered as dirty, nasty and forbidden and the child would cease to regard its own impulses, and therefore itself, as nasty and dirty and would not feel guilty about its bodily urges.

It is natural to love one's child but it is very difficult indeed to do so if you cannot love yourself. It is also very difficult to tell a parent to have pleasure in the natural functions of the child if the parent has unconscious fears and inhibitions about his own natural functions. While the intellect is a poor and limited instrument to break through the deep-seated taboos and compulsions, it nevertheless can help transform innate predispositions by first making them conscious and by encouraging new attitudes. A start has to be made.

The satisfaction of the erotogenic zones in children depends to a large extent upon the sexual genital satisfactions of the parents, for should they suffer from sexual frustrations and inhibitions, then their attitudes to the child's pre-genital sexuality would be disturbed. So if parents want their children to be healthy and happy they must endeavour to have a happy sex life. The parents' sexual happiness is of great concern to the child. No child can be happy or fulfilled if the parents are sexually unhappy. Sexual happiness is thus a duty to the child. (I am extremely conscious of the wry smiles this imperative will evoke in many people, but I am in a hurry, we are all in a hurry, so let us just tell the truth. It might help.)

Besides the gratification of the child's erotogenic zones and the respect for infantile sexual needs there is the major problem of the genital sexuality of children. It is here that patriarchal attitudes have their major impact upon the psychic structure. We have seen that there are a number of genital primacies in children during which they experience genital sexual needs, at the ages of two, five and thirteen, roughly speaking. The question arises: how are parents to deal with them? As I intend here merely to provide some pointers towards a new attitude, let us take just a few aspects of the problem.

Freud has drawn our attention to the importance of the "primal scene", i.e. the child's observation of parental intercourse and the emotional upheaval this creates in the child. From about the age of two years the child is extremely curious about sex and conscious of its parents' sexual activities. (This usually arouses disbelief in many people, even during psychoanalysis, but there are almost always memories, usually repressed, about the child's impression of parental sexuality.) What attitude are parents to take towards the child witnessing their sexual relations? First of all the father must accept that the boy wants his wife sexually and the mother must accept that her daughter wants her husband sexually. Of course it would be impossible for a child of two or five

14. CONCLUSIONS AND BEGINNINGS

years to have intercourse with the parent of the opposite sex, but there are compensations – nature has seen to that. For instance, if the boy knows that his father has intercourse with mother and if he further knows that father does not mind the boy's excitement and arousal on observing it, then the boy can identify with his father and take a vicarious pleasure in the act. Above all, he can masturbate without guilt or anxiety, and in this way participate in his father's pleasure. This presupposes that the father is not afraid either of his own sexuality or of the sexual arousal of his son, that he does not fear his son as a rival.

There is no need for any ostentatious display of freedom or for anxious avoidance of traumatising the child. If the child is in the same room with his parents in a cot then some sign of acknowledgement of the child, some sign of open enjoyment and of acceptance of the child's libido (while he is listening wide awake with his eyes closed or half-closed) suffices to allay any anxiety or guilt in the child. People would be surprised to know how sensitive a child is about the parents' attitude towards it in matters of sex and what impact subtle and unspoken expressions of attitudes can have upon it. The father could acknowledge the boy's sexuality, not be embarrassed, the mother not be too coy to caress the child.

On the other hand, over-stimulation of the child is also not desirable. For instance the mother should not play with his genitals but should accept and acknowledge his genital arousal with good humour. The acceptance of his sexuality is all-important to the little boy. Masturbation should of course be accepted and respected.

With girls the matter is not very different. Most little girls are left ignorant of the existence of their vagina, the mother never, *but never*, talks about it. That does not mean that girls do not feel sensations in their vagina; on the contrary, there is every evidence that they experience as much stimulation in their genitals as boys do. They often experience the equivalent of a boy's erection in vaginal spasms but these are invariably referred to as tummy pains or cramps and never for what they really are. There is much mystification of the tummy as some secret area where unmentionable things happen besides the ordinary digestive processes and the child quickly realises that vaginal sensations are not to be mentioned or acknowledged, in fact, are not supposed to be there. So while the girl is not supposed to have an internal genital she cannot help having genital sensations. No wonder that the child soon feels guilty and embarrassed by sensations that are not acknowledged as belonging to an internal organ. She learns to hide her sexuality, she becomes nonplussed and confused about it and she gets the impression that her femininity is unacceptable. No wonder then that she becomes envious of the penis. She feels that a boy's sexuality is accepted while hers is not.

The whole syndrome of feminine shyness, secretiveness, guilt and sense of inadequacy, the whole picture of some mysterious sinfulness about femininity is here engendered to become a cultural characteristic of the woman. Of course as with the boy there can be compensatory processes if a girl is shown love and affection. Not all girls grow up stunted and blocked as persons, and it is indeed one of the miracles of human adaptability that, despite the enormous psycho-sexual handicap imposed upon girls in our culture, many develop into healthy, beautiful and intelligent beings. But the hardship of the non-recognition of the girl's sexuality as a child is responsible for a large number of neuroses and illnesses in women. Not realising that there is an organ behind her little opening, many girls grow up with fears of the penis, with notions of violence and injury in sex, or with masochistic fantasies of having to be injured in order to experience sexual pleasures. The rape fantasies so prevalent in women are not merely an expression of sexual needs for which they do not wish to be held responsible but they are very often associated with pain and violence and the masochistic component creates considerable guilt and anxiety. Another aspect of this lack of acknowledgement of her own vagina is the assumption of passivity in the woman, her sense of dependency upon the male's sexual activity and the resulting envy and resentment against him on the one hand and submissiveness on the other. In fact the vagina is every bit as active sexually as the penis but its activity is not as obvious as that of a penis and if it is repressed from consciousness can only show itself in a whole host of neurotic and somatic disturbances, hysterias and a high incidence of hypochondria in

14. CONCLUSIONS AND BEGINNINGS

women. It is astonishing how many grown-up women remain ignorant of their vagina, are, as it were, unfamiliar with it, and how often they consider it as unacceptable, unattractive and something to be denied.

It is of the utmost importance that parents realise that a girl has a great need for genital acknowledgement. They should refer to her vagina, should signal to her verbally and pre-verbally that she has an important sexual organ behind her opening, they should look at it on those many occasions when the girl opens her legs and invites attention. The exhibitionistic urges of girls are more highly developed than those of the boy for the simple reason that she needs more reassurance that the hidden vagina is noticed, accepted and loved. Parents who do not acknowledge the little girl's sexuality castrate her and make her feel inadequate for life.

Nakedness in families and in groups of children should be accepted as a matter of course in situations where nakedness is *functional and natural*. The curiosity aroused by natural nakedness should be fully respected and explanations of the differences between the sexes given at the earliest possible time. Sexual exploration between children should be fully accepted and even encouraged as a form of learning and discovery and the beauty of the genitals, male and female, conveyed to them. If people only knew what a traumatic experience it is for a boy to discover an opening between the girl's legs when he expects a penis there, having no idea that she has a genital of her own inside! Freud observed that the absence of a penis in a girl arouses the boy's castration anxieties, he imagines her to be a castrated boy. Moreover, as he does not know that a woman has a receptive organ, his urge to penetrate her will arouse sadistic fantasies of cutting her open, forcing himself into her and injuring her. At the same time he will feel guilty about the aggressive aspect of his sexuality. He will project some of his aggression upon the woman who will then be seen by him not only as a victim but also as a threat. In his fantasies he will imagine her genital as a crab, as pincers or scissors which are likely to injure his penis. (Some men never get over this impression, remain terrified of women sexually and become homosexuals.)

When the vagina is acknowledged as an organ that receives without hurt or pain, and its own desires are recognised, then the boy's penis is not a threatening and threatened object but an organ which gives pleasure to the girl and receives pleasure from her; then both penis and vagina are good objects embracing and intermingling with each other. There is no possible reason, apart from irrational anxiety, why sexual play between children from four or five onwards should be inhibited. Let parents be assured that if sexual curiosity and play is accepted as natural and beautiful, there would be no compulsion about it amongst children, unlike the hidden compulsions of sexual fantasies and symptoms so prevalent in our time.

If the girl's vaginal sexuality gains full recognition then the periods of vaginal repression and clitoral primacy would be reduced and there would be far less conflict between the two sexualities of women. There would be much less penis envy among girls and castration anxiety among boys. The vagina is not merely a passive-submissive but an active-receptive organ with an embracing and incorporative sexuality as distinct from the pushing, penetrative sexuality of the boy. As an embracing receptive being, the woman has many psychological characteristics which are different from those of the male, but these differences are complementary to each other and are not competitive.

Another aspect to be noticed here is that when the woman's vagina is given conscious attention in the formative years, then female cultural symbols will emerge: a female dimension will develop in our culture to complement the male cultural symbols which have, up till now, been dominant. Women would again develop their divinities, their principles and ideas in a recognisable manner as distinct cultural entities, and it is high time that this should happen if we are to be saved from the aggressive mania of the male Gods.

There have been great advances in the liberation of sexual relationships between young people. However, the important thing to remember is that up till now young people have had to fight for their sexual rights against parents and authorities: they feel a kind of persecution mania, are convinced that they engage in sexuality against parental authority, and often will do so in a spirit

14. CONCLUSIONS AND BEGINNINGS

of defiance to affirm their independence and identity. Now, parental approval of a child's sexuality is important not only in infancy and childhood but particularly during the sexual puberty of adolescence. It is only when parents can feel pleasure in their children's sexual pleasure and can communicate it to them that young people will feel free to enjoy their sexuality rather than use sexuality as a kind of rebellion against their parents. If sexuality is used by adolescents as a weapon with which to fight authority, then their sexuality acquires an aggressive quality and will lose much of its spontaneity. If parents communicate sexual acceptance and instil sexual confidence in their children, then there is little fear that their sexuality will become compulsive. Nature has provided the rhythms of excitement and relaxation, and intellectual and cultural activities would not suffer from free sexuality in adolescence. It may be that a different kind of culture will emerge – new symbols taking the place of the old. One must have a measure of trust in the future and in any case there is an urgent need for new cultural symbols and ideas.

How does an affirmative attitude by parents to their own and to the child's libido affect the Oedipus complex? If the father does not play the role of sexual repressor then the boy will, to a large extent, cease to be afraid of his own sexual impulses and pleasure sensations. He will become less angry and aggressive, he will project less anger and aggression upon the father, father will not symbolise a forbidding and punishing object that, in turn, arouses the child's fear and anger. The child will not see father as a punishing castrating figure and he will not want to kill him. The boy will not stand in awe and trembling before father, he will not have to propitiate him and restitute him in worship, he will not have to glorify him into an omnipotent Godhead, he will not be impelled to project his own aggressive urges upon the members of other tribes and nations, and he will not have to fight them in order to defend father. He will cease to be paranoid, constantly seeing his God and his State threatened by the 'others'; he will not feel the need to wave a flag carrying father's image aloft and fight for it in the rituals of war and self-sacrifice.

Patriarchal totem worship of state and authority would become meaningless. When people feel acknowledged and accepted as persons then they will accept and acknowledge others as persons and not merely as members of other tribes or nations. When people are not made to feel guilty for their human needs then they can recognise the humanity of others.

The attitude to women would change. They would not have to be conquered. As sexuality would be an overtly accepted part of the life of an individual, so women would be individuals to whom one would relate according to one's own and her wishes without sin or compulsive ceremonials imposed from above. People would do their own choosing in sexual matters without the need for moral justification. This in turn would make the religious or State sanction for marriage unnecessary, and true marriage, the marriage based on love and the will of two people could take place. People would either love each other or they would not, and they would live together or they would not, according to their own feelings and their own choice. Indeed, there would be no compulsion to imagine eternal love in a sexual attraction, no need to guarantee life-long fidelity. While sexuality would not be desirable without affection there would be no need to swear immortal love. Love goes beyond sexual attraction but of course includes it. It relates to the mind, the body, the thoughts and the personality of the other person and pulls people inexorably to each other and makes them want to be together. This is marriage – to share in each other's experiences, to discover the other and oneself in the other every day and to need this mutual discovery and sharing of experience. For this no contracts and no State sanctions are required.

But what about the family? If sex is not a sin or a source of anxiety, if love is not destroyed when sexual attraction towards another person occurs occasionally, then the coercive bonds of religion or state are not necessary. There would be no need for protective walls around the family. On the other hand the family would have to continue to exist just as long as the world outside is strange and hostile. The abolition of the family, in our sense, demands the creation of a society of non-alienated people; a society where people relate to each other without fear or mistrust, where sexuality, affections, pleasure and work and a sense of responsibility draw people together in comradeship, where every

14. CONCLUSIONS AND BEGINNINGS

man is a creator and a source of pleasure to himself and to others.

When the patriarchal compulsions of mistrust and fear are overcome people can see themselves creatively engaged in the co-operative enterprise of making a human environment and of living in it; in other words where groups of free people can share in their work activities with no owners and slaves, no kings and authorities to exploit them and repress them. Then families can disappear because children can be members of a large group without being tied to their parents but related to them by natural needs and inclinations, while other members of the community or group would in some measure share in the parents' affection for the children. I do not think that parenthood and parental love for the children would disappear, but I do think that children would have a wider circle of friends, uncles and aunts, brothers and sisters, to whom they could relate. The sharing in the care of children would be natural in such a society, and would facilitate the sharing of the means of production.

The elimination of the Oedipus complex would do away with the authoritarian and hierarchic compulsions and pave the way for a society of communalism of which, up till now, we have only the vaguest notions and which we all too often declare to be impossible in reality, relating it to the dream world of a heavenly existence. Who in the massed, mingled, apprehensive collective existence that is modern society still perceives what community is? As Martin Buber has written: "Community is the being no longer side by side but *with* one another of a multitude of persons. And this multitude experiences everywhere a turning to, a dynamic facing of, the others, a flowing from I to Thou."[2] Only when there is an *I–Thou* relationship between persons can we speak of *we*.

The ego, the self that can relate itself to other selves directly, as it were, could dispense with the old superego. The superego would be replaced by an ego-ideal that affirms the autonomy of men's humanity without the need for an internal and superhuman watchman to guard us against the libido. Just as the old superego has found its embodiment in authoritarian society, so the new human ego ideal would find its embodiment in a society which affirms man's pleasure in himself and in others, which would actualise man's freedom towards himself in the freedom of men to each other. The construction of such a society is necessary if we are to overcome the compulsions towards destruction which our civilisation produces. It is also possible, however strange this may seem to armoured and repressed people. Modern technology with its advances in automation and miniaturisation will make the hierarchical mass societies unnecessary and facilitate productive processes which are suited for a communalistic social structure. Furthermore, the liberation of the libido from its age-old negations would eliminate the compulsive need for substitute gratifications that has to be satisfied by a proliferation of commodities. The consumer psychology which was inevitable to alienated and repressed individuals will be seen as a pathological manifestation of a culture that has denied man his primary gratifications, that has estranged him from the sources of pleasure and joy that are innate to him.

While a detailed analysis of the politics of a non-patriarchal society does not fall within the scope of this book, it is imperative to realise that the social revolution is a dimension of the sexual revolution – that the two are interwoven and the one is not possible without the other.

There is a self-destructive drive in mankind which invades all institutions and ideologies. This is a fact which both the trauma of living in this century as well as the investigations of Freud have made abundantly clear. But this drive does not need to be seen as a divine force – Thanatos. It is a consequence of the thwarting of instincts, a secondary and not a primary drive, however deep-seated and central it is to the human condition. It has to be taken very seriously. It is almost all-powerful. But it can be conquered and only Eros can conquer it. If we cannot love we are condemned to hate, and if we can love we have no disposition to hate – it is as simple as that.

1. Georg Lukacs: *History and Class Consciousness* (Merlin Press, 1971).
2. Martin Buber: *Between Man and Man* (Fontana Library, 1969).

Selected Bibliography

Abraham, Karl: *Selected Papers on Psychoanalysis*, Hogarth, 1955.
— *Clinical Papers and Essays on Psychoanalysis*, Hogarth, 1955.
Adorno, T. H. et al: *The Authoritarian Personality*, W. W. Norton & Co., 1969.
Alexander, Franz: *Psychoanalysis and Psychotherapy*, Allen & Unwin, 1957.
Bachofen, J. J: *Myth, Religion and Mother Right*, Princeton University Press, 1973.
Boadella, David: *Wilhelm Reich: The Evolution of His Work*, Vision Press, 1973.
Bonaparte, Marie: *Female Sexuality*, Hogarth Press, 1951.
Brecher, E. M: *The Sex Researchers*, Panther Books, 1972.
Briffault, Robert: *The Mothers*, London, George Allen & Unwin, 1960.
Brown, N. O: *Life Against Death*, Sphere Books, 1968.
Buber, Martin: *Between Man and Man*, Fontana Library, 1961.
Cassirer, Ernst: *Language and Myth*, Harper & Bros., 1946.
Chomsky, Noam: A Review of Skinner's 'Verbal Behaviour', *Language* 35 (1), pp. 26–58, 1959.
Cipolla, Carlo M: *The Economic History of World Population*, Pelican Books, 1965.
Comfort, Alex: *Nature and Human Nature*, Pelican Books, 1969.
— *Sex in Society*, Pelican Books, 1964.
Dasman, R. F: *Planet in Peril?*, Penguin Books / Unesco, 1972.
Deutsch, Helene: *The Psychology of Women: A Psychoanalytic Interpretation*, New York, Grune & Stratton, 1945.
Deutscher, Isaac: *Stalin*, New York, Vintage Books, 1960.
Dubos, R: *So Human an Animal*, Rupert Hart Davis, 1970.
Durkheim, Emile: *The Elementary Forms of Religious Life*, Allen & Unwin, 1965.
Ehrlich, Paul R: *The Population Bomb*, Pan Books, 1971.
Engels, Friedrich: *The Origin of the Family, Private Property and the State*, Harmondsworth, Penguin, 1985.

English, O. Spurgeon, and Pearson, G. H: *Emotional Problems of Living*, Allen & Unwin, 1965.
Erikson, Erik H: *Childhood and Society*, London, Vintage, 1995.
— *Identity, Youth and Crisis*, Faber & Faber, 1968.
Fenichel, Otto: *The Psychoanalytic Theory of Neuroses*, Routledge & Kegan Paul, 1955.
Ferenczi, S: *Further Contributions to the Theory and Technique of Psychoanalysis*, Hogarth Press, 1955.
— *Final Contributions to the Problems and Methods of Psychoanalysis*, Hogarth 1955.
Firestone, Shulamith: *The Dialectic of Sex*, Paladin, 1972.
Frankfort, Henri, *Kingship and the Gods,* Chicago, 1948.
Frankl, George: *The End of War or the End of Mankind*, London, Globe Publications, 1955.
— *The Failure of the Sexual Revolution*, London, Kahn & Averill, 1974; New English Library, 1975; Open Gate Press, 2003.
— *The Social History of the Unconscious – A Psychoanalysis of Society*, Open Gate Press, 1989, 2003.
  Also published in two volumes, as:
    Archaeology of the Mind, Open Gate Press, 1990, 1992, 2002.
    Civilisation: Utopia and Tragedy, Open Gate Press, 1990, 1992, 2002.
— *The Unknown Self*, Open Gate Press, 1990, 1993, 2001.
— *Exploring the Unconscious*, Open Gate Press, 1994, 2001.
— *Foundations of Morality*, Open Gate Press, 2000, 2001.
— *Blueprint for a Sane Society*, Open Gate Press, 2003.
Frankl, Victor E: *The Will to Meaning* – An Introduction to Logotherapy, Souvenir Press, 1971.
— *Psychotherapy and Existentialism*, Souvenir Press, 1971.
Freud, Anna: *The Ego and the Mechanisms of Defence*, Hogarth Press, 1937.
Freud, Sigmund: 1905 *Three Essays on the Theory of Sexuality*, S. E. Vol. 7.
— 1915-17 *Introductory Lectures on Psychoanalysis*, S. E. Vol.15-16.
— 1927 *The Future of an Illusion*, S. E. Vol. 21.
— 1930 *Civilisation and Its Discontents*, S. E. Vol. 21.
— 1933 *New Introductory Lectures on Psychoanalysis*, S. E. Vol. 22.
Fromm, Erich: *The Sane Society*, Routledge, 1991.
— *The Crisis of Psychoanalysis*, Jonathan Cape, 1971.
Gellner, E: *Words and Things*. An examination of, and attack on, Linguistic Philosophy, Routledge & Kegan Paul, 1979.

Goldmann, Lucien: *The Human Sciences and Philosophy*, London, Jonathan Cape, 1969.
Greer, Germaine: *The Female Eunuch*, Paladin, 1971.
Holbrook, David: *Pseudo Revolution*, Tom Stacey, 1972.
Horkheimer, Max and Adorno, Theodor: *Dialectic of Enlightenment*, Allen Lane, 1973.
Howells, William White: *Mankind in the Making*, Pelican, 1970.
Jung, Carl Gustav: *Symbols of Transformation*, Routledge & Kegan Paul, 1952.
Kant, Immanuel: *Critique of Pure Reason*, Dent, 1969.
— *Foundation of the Metaphysic of Morals*, New York, 1959.
Klein, Melanie: *The Psychoanalysis of Children*, Hogarth, 1964.
Koestler, A: *The Act of Creation*, Pan Books, 1964.
— *The Ghost in the Machine*, Hutchinson, 1967.
Kolakowski, Leszek: *Marxism and Beyond*, Paladin, 1971.
Kollontai, Alexandra: *Autobiography of a Sexually Emancipated Woman*, Orbach & Chambers, 1972.
Kropotkin, Peter: *Mutual Aid*, Pelican Books, 1939.
Kuhn, T: *The Structure of Scientific Revolutions*, Chicago, 1962.
Lévi-Strauss, Claude: *Structural Anthropology*, Basic Books, 1963.
Lichtheim, George: *Marxism*, Routledge & Kegan Paul, 1977.
Lukacs, Georg: *History and Class Consciousness*, Merlin Press, 1971.
Luxemburg, Rosa: *The Russian Revolution*, Ann Arbor, 1961.
Malinowski, B. K: *Sex and Repression in Savage Society*, Routledge & Kegan Paul, 1979.
Marcuse, Herbert: *One Dimensional Man*, Routledge, 1991.
— *Eros and Civilization*, Ark, 1987.
Marx, Karl: *Economic and Philosophic Manuscripts*, Lawrence & Wishart, 1963.
— *Grundrisse*, edited by David McLellan, Macmillan, 1971.
— and Engels, Friedrich: *The German Ideology*, Lawrence & Wishart, The Collected Works, Vol.5.
Masters, W. H. and Johnson, V. E: *Human Sexual Response*, Churchill, 1966.
May, Rollo: *Love and Will*, Fontana, 1972.
Mead, Margaret: *Coming of Age in Samoa*, Penguin, 1977.
Meszaros, I: *Marx's Theory of Alienation*, Merlin Press, 1970.
Millett, Kate: *Sexual Politics*, Abacus, 1972.
Mumford, Lewis: *The Conduct of Life*, Secker & Warburg, 1952.
— *The Myth of the Machine*, Secker & Warburg, 1967.

SELECTED BIBLIOGRAPHY

Nietzsche, Friedrich: *Genealogy of Morals*, Doubleday & Co., 1956.
— *The Birth of Tragedy*, Doubleday & Co., 1956.
Packard, Vance: *The Sexual Wilderness*, Pan Books, 1966.
Popper, Karl: *The Open Society and Its Enemies*, Routledge, 1966.
Praz, Mario: *The Romantic Agony*, Oxford University Press, 1951.
Reich, Wilhelm: *Character Analysis*, Vision Press, 1951.
— *The Mass Psychology of Fascism*, Farrar, Straus, Giroux, 1980.
— *The Function of the Orgasm*, Panther Books, 1966.
— *The Sexual Revolution*, Vision Press, 1972.
Reik, Theodor: *Myth and Guilt*, Hutchinson, 1958.
— *Ritual. Psychoanalytic Studies*, New York, Grove Press, 1962.
Riesman, David: *The Lonely Crowd*, New Haven, 1950.
Rivers, W. H. R: 'Medicine, Magic and Religion' (The Fitzpatrick Lectures 1915/16), Routledge, 2001.
Robinson, Paul A: *The Sexual Radicals*, Paladin, 1972.
Roheim, G: *Psychoanalysis and Anthropology*, New York, International Universities Press, 1950.
— *The Riddle of the Sphinx*, Hogarth Press, 1934.
Russell, Bertrand: *Has Man a Future?* Allen & Unwin, 1961.
— *Marriage and Morals*, Liveright, 1970.
Sartre, Jean-Paul: *Existentialism and Humanism*, Methuen, 1970.
Saugstad, Per: *An Enquiry into the Foundations of Psychology*, Allen & Unwin, 1965.
Skinner, B. F: *The Behaviour of Organisms*, New York, Appleton, 1938.
— *Verbal Behaviour*, Appleton, 1957.
Sorokin, P. A: *Society, Culture and Personality*, Harper's Social Studies Series, 1947.
— *The Reconstruction of Humanity*, Boston, Harper & Row, 1966.
Tawney, R. H: *Religion and the Rise of Capitalism*, Pelican, 1940.
Trotsky, Leon: *The Revolution Betrayed*, Doubleday & Co., 1937.
Tucker, Robert: *Philosophy and Myth in Karl Marx*, Cambridge University Press, 1961.
Weber, Max: *The Protestant Ethic and the Spirit of Capitalism*, Routledge, 2001.
Whitehead, A. N: *Adventures of Ideas*, Pelican Books, 1948.

Index

A

Abraham, Karl viii, 31, 131, 144
Adler, Victor vii
Adorno, Theodor 49
Aggression 24, 32, 37, 38, 43, 97, 131, 133, 136, 137, 140, 143, 160, 169, 171
Alienation 8, 9, 10, 11, 13, 14, 15, 17, 29, 40, 123, 124, 152, 157, 170, 172, 173
Anxiety 5, 14, 24, 25, 95, 133, 167, 174
— pleasure anxiety 25, 32, 128, 173
Armour 25, 117, 119, 127, 130, 143, 169
Art 162
Authoritarianism 7, 18, 29, 41, 117, 138, 157, 173

B

Baudelaire, Charles 90, 99
Behaviourist psychology 12, 124, 130
Bernheim, H. 22
Bi-sexuality 153, 162
Blake, William 93
Brecher, Edward M. 130, 133
Brecher, Ruth 133
Breuer, Dr Josef 22
Brophy, Brigid 57
Brunswick, Dr Ruth Mack 155
Brustein, Robert 2, 5
Buber, Martin 183, 184
Byron, Lord George 89, 90, 93, 94, 95, 99, 101

C

Capital 9, 11, 13, 41, 48
Capitalism vii, xi, 8, 14, 15, 18, 40, 41, 81, 138, 156
Charcot, Jean-Martin 22
Christianity 46, 86, 90, 135
Civilisation 39
Comfort, Alex 102
Commerce 78
Commodity 78
Communalism 183, 184
Communism xiii, 138
Cosmopolitan 60, 63, 64, 65, 70, 72, 112
Conquest, Robert 104
Croce, Benedetto 98

D

Dante Alighieri 90, 91, 92
Death wish viii
Descartes, René 21, 26
Deutsch, Helene 60, 155
Devil 35, 86
Dewey, John 12
Dichter, Dr Ernest 55, 56, 78
Dickson, Ruth 61, 78
Don Juan 94, 167
Drives vii, xi, 23, 83
Drugs 46, 47

E

Ego xi, xii, 21, 26, 27, 28, 30, 51, 83, 122, 129, 130, 172, 183
Engels, Friedrich 15, 18, 155
Enlightenment 3
Eros 47, 48, 157, 184

INDEX

Esalen Institute 114
Eve 95
Exhibitionism 108, 114
Existentialists 5, 82, 124
Externalisation 6, 11, 40

F

Fenichel, Otto 131
Faust 94
Firestone, Shulamith 76, 141, 142, 143
Flaubert, Gustave 90
Forum 60, 105, 108, 114
Frankl, Victor 82, 123
Free association 23
Freedom 171, 172, 174, 184
Freud, Anna 155
Freud, Sigmund xiii, 5, 19, 20, 30, 32, 21, 22, 23, 24, 25, 26, 60, 61, 68, 69, 109, 126, 131, 142, 144, 145, 148, 149, 152, 153, 155, 158, 174, 176, 179, 184
— and infantile sexuality 23, 82
— *New Introductory Lectures on Psychoanalysis* 153–154, 158
— and 'primal scene' 176
Fromm, Erich 13

G

Galileo 3
Gautier, Theophile 99
Gay Liberation Front 76
Genet, Jean 149
Gide, André 99
Good Housekeeping 68
Goethe, Johann Wolfgang 89, 99
Greer, Germaine 147, 156, 158, 163, 164
Guilt 41, 42, 108, 114, 131, 134, 159, 174, 175

H

Harpers & Queen 53, 54, 57, 65
Hartogs, Renatus 63
Hegel, Georg Friedrich 3, 16, 40
Hess, Moses 17
Holbrook, David 82
Hollander, Xaviera 104
Honey 73, 74, 75, 76, 77, 78
Hopson, Charlotte 59

I

Id 21, 27, 28, 30, 33, 38
Impotence 159, 161, 169
In Depth 115
Inhibition 25, 127, 129, 130, 131, 173, 175
Intra 108, 115
Inglis, Ruth 57
It 116
IT 121

J

Janet, Pierre 22
Janus 108, 115
Jaspers, Karl 14
Jehovah 89, 92
Jesus 41
Jew 37
Jonson, Ben 136
Journalism 51, 52
Jung, C. G. 82

K

Kant, Immanuel xiii, 3, 6, 8, 16, 19, 20, 21, 28
Keats, John 90, 99
Keay, Douglas 62
Kierkegaard, Soren 21
Kinsey, A. C. 147, 149, 159
Klein, Melanie 31, 144, 155
Knave 106
Koestler, Arthur 171
Kollontai, Alexandra 138

L

La Belle Dame sans Merci 90, 95, 121
Lampl de Groot, Dr J. 155
Latency period 144, 145
Lawrence, D. H. 71, 166
Lenin, Vladimir Ilyich 3, 18
Lesbianism 76, 136, 146
Libido xii, 24, 25, 32, 34, 39, 45, 47, 83, 84, 88, 89, 97, 99, 100, 119, 133, 141, 143, 144, 150, 170, 173, 174, 175, 183, 184
Lichtheim, George 28
Lilith 96, 100, 112, 136
Locke, John 21
Look Now 75
Love xiv, 90, 99, 171, 172
Lovelace, Ralph Milbanke, Earl of 93
Lukacs, Georg 172, 184
Luxemburg, Rosa 18, 138

M

McDermott, Sandra 61
Machine 12, 14
Mailer, Norman 139
Malinowski, Bronislaw viii, 155, 162
Mallarmé, Etienne (Stéphane) 90
Marcuse, Herbert 48, 49, 81
Marx, Karl xiii, 3, 5, 7, 8, 9, 10, 11, 13, 14, 15, 16, 17, 18, 19, 29, 39, 40, 41, 45, 155, 157
Marxism 3, 14, 16
— Marxist xi, 10, 17
Masochism 89, 91, 95, 96, 115, 161
Masters and Johnson 58, 61, 125, 126, 127, 128, 129, 130, 132, 147, 149, 151
Masturbation 125, 126, 132, 149, 177

Mater dolorosa 90
Matriarchy 88, 89
May, Rollo 82, 167, 168
Mayfair 110
Mead, Margaret 162
Mephisto 35
Messianic 16, 17
Miller, Henry 139, 140, 141
Millett, Kate 76
Milton, John 93, 158
Mind vii, 7, 8, 13, 21, 25, 129, 130
— mind/body problem 26
Modern Man 111
Monotheism 134
Morality xi, 7, 8, 37
Muscular rigidity 25, 85, 86, 126, 127, 132
Mysticism 3, 49, 50

N

Napoleon 22
Narcissism 130, 155, 164, 165
Nazism vii
Necrophilia 118, 140
Neurosis 22, 28, 131, 169, 172
Neves, Vivian 64
Neville, Richard 117, 120
Nietzsche, Friedrich 21, 35, 99
'19' 75, 78
Nova 56, 57, 58, 59, 60, 64, 70, 72, 76
Novalis, Friedrich 21

O

Oedipus complex 6, 31, 35, 36, 85, 155, 163, 164, 173, 174, 181, 183
— Oedipal conflict 88
— Oedipal guilt 144
Orgasm 61, 62, 110, 111, 112, 113, 115, 125, 126, 128, 130, 131, 132, 133, 149, 150, 167,

INDEX

170
— orgasmic spasm 132, 151
Orwell, George 171
Oz 116, 117, 118, 119, 120, 121

P
Pan 35
Paranoia 30, 131, 148, 170, 173
Patriarchy viii, 85, 88, 89, 95, 100, 109, 129, 134, 135, 139, 157, 173, 174
Pavlov, Ivan 123
Penis envy 145, 152, 155, 177, 180
Penthouse 102, 103, 104, 105, 106, 110, 114
Perversions 115, 170
Petrarch, Francesco 90, 92
Petticoat 76
Picasso, Pablo 35
Playboy 102, 103, 104, 105
Pleasure 175, 177, 181, 182, 184
— pleasure anxiety viii, 25, 31, 32
— pleasure principle 30
Popper, Karl 16
Pornography xiii, 54, 79–87, 101
— commercial pornography 102, 106, 140
— political pornography 116, 140
Praz, Mario 93, 101
Probe 111, 115
Procreation 85, 160
Projection 32, 33, 35, 37, 38, 173
Prometheus 47
Prostitutes (*see also* whores) 126
Protagoras 5
Protestant 41
Psychoanalysis xii, 19, 32, 123, 124, 153, 166, 176
Psychology 130
— depth psychology 19

Psychosis 28, 33
Puritanism 46

R
Rabelais, François 35
Radicalism xii, xiii, 1, 3, 5, 6, 7, 19, 49, 142, 157, 173
Rambout of Orange 91
Raskolnikov 94
Rationalism 2, 6
Reality vii, 8, 19, 20, 21, 27, 28, 39
Reason 1, 2, 3, 4, 7, 20, 21
Regression 84, 100, 140
Reich, Wilhelm viii, ix, xii, xiv, 19, 24, 26, 43, 60, 61, 80, 81, 87, 108, 110, 116, 117, 121, 126, 127, 128, 129, 131, 133, 138, 146, 150, 155, 169, 171
Reik, Theodor 131
Repression xiii, 22, 23, 26, 42, 83, 84, 129, 133, 147, 155, 157, 173
Richthofen, Frieda von 166
Roheim, Geza viii
Romanticism 88–101
Roth, Philip
— Alexander Portnoy 167, 168
— Dr Spielvogel 168
Rougemont, Denis de 90, 101
Rudel, Geoffrey 91
Russell, Bertrand 35
Russia vii, 138
Russian Revolution xii

S
Sade, Marquis de 90, 95
Sadism 89, 91, 95, 97, 100, 115, 118, 119, 131, 139, 140, 141
Sappho 76
Satan 92, 93
Satanism 140
Schiller, Friedrich 93, 99

Schizophrenia 32, 50
Schopenhauer, Arthur 20, 21
Science 122, 123, 124, 131
Search 115
Sexual revolution ix, xi, xii, xiii, 13, 43, 44, 45, 48, 49, 50, 54, 55, 77, 82, 170, 173, 184
— industry 45, 49
— liberation viii
— repression viii, xii, 23, 43, 49, 81, 122, 129, 130, 131, 134, 137, 155, 170, 171
She 70, 72, 78
Shelley, Percy B. 93
Shepard, Dr Martin 114
Sherfey, Dr Mary Jane 148, 149, 150, 151
Sin 89, 182
Smith, Anthony 58
Social revolution 173, 184
— social structures vii
Society:
— authoritarian society viii, xi, 18, 41, 44, 79, 137
— matriarchal society 86
— patriarchal society 6
Sociology 51, 52
Spender, Stephen 54
Splitting xiii, 32, 173
Stalin, Josef 3, 18, 69, 138
Stalinism xii
Stekel, Wilhelm 60, 110
Suck 116
Superego xiii, 28, 29, 30, 31, 32, 38, 41, 42, 49, 51, 97, 108, 114, 117, 136, 140, 141, 157, 171, 183
Swinburne, Algernon Charles 90, 96, 98, 99, 101

Symbolisation 27, 32, 33, 39, 84
Symptoms xi, 20, 22, 23, 82, 84, 131

T
Taboo 82, 95, 108, 132, 172, 173
Taylor, Dr Howard C. 127
Thanatos 47, 157, 184
Tristan and Isolde 90
Trotskyites vii, 116
Troubadours 90, 91
Tucker, Robert 16

U
Unconscious 19, 20, 21, 22, 23, 27, 31, 34, 39, 82, 83, 173, 175
Unisex 161, 164, 165, 166

V
Vagina 143, 144, 145, 146, 147, 152, 177, 178, 179, 180
Vincent, Sally 57
Vogue 54

W
War 39, 181
Wells, H. G. 134
White, Cynthia L. 53, 72, 78
Whores 57, 85, 86
Wilde, Oscar 90, 99
Will 13, 20, 21
Witch 35
Woman 65, 67, 68, 70, 71, 72, 77
Woman's Own 55, 56, 68, 70, 71, 72
Woman's Weekly 71, 72
Women's liberation xiii, 112, 113, 136, 137, 139, 157, 162, 164